MW00512575

Energy Healing Application

Energy Healing Initiation and Steps, Levels of Energy
Healing, Learning to Read the Energy

Michael MacKay

TABLE OF CONTENTS

Introduction 13

Chapter 1 The Definition of Healing 15

What is Energy? 15

The Energy Body 18

Chapter 2 Energy Healing.. 22

The Reiki Story... 22

What do Energy Healers do? 26

Our Dynamic Multilayer Energy Field 28

Scientific Studies That Prove That Energy Healing Works.................... 29

When Will Energy Healing Help Me? 36

Chapter 3 Levels of Energy Healing 39

Different Established Energy Healing Modalities 39

The principles of Energy Healing.. 40

Being Connected to the Energy Field Awareness 42

Principle 1 - Don't be Angry... 42

Principle 2 - Do not Worry... 43

Principle 3 - Be Filled with Gratitude 43

Principle 4 - Work Hard 44

Principle 5 - Be Kind to Others... 44

Primary Awareness Exercise.. 45

Energy Healing Practices 45

Meditation... 46

Osho Philosophy 47

Awakening the Body Response... 50

Deep Touch... 51

Deep Wave 52

Deep Sound 52

Deep Gymnastics 53

Chapter 4 Energy Healing Initiation and Steps 54

    Ryoho 54

    Initiation 57

    Steps 59

    The first step 61

    The second step 62

    The third step 63

    The fourth step 64

    Circle Training 65

    Oral Tradition 66

    Reiki Symbols 67

    1st character 70

    2nd character 70

    3rd character 71

    4th character 71

Chapter 5 Learning to Read the Energy Field 72

    Energy movement and the Chakra 73

    Unlocking and Balancing the Chakras 73

    When energy is Unbalanced or Blocked? 74

    Is there a universal practice for unlocking chakras? 76

    First Chakra 76

    Second Chakra 77

    Third Chakra 78

    Fourth Chakra 79

    Fifth Chakra 79

    Sixth Chakra 80

    Seventh Chakra 81

Chapter 6 The Chakra Meditation Opening Chakras in Meditation 83

    Effects of Chakra Meditation 86

Things to note 87

Chapter 7 Energy Healing Application 90

Hand Positions for Energy Healing.. 90

The fourth position - Hands cover the neck 91

The fifth position - Hands just above the chest, at heart level........... 91

The sixth position - Hands at the level of the solar plexus.............. 91

The seventh position - Hands on the stomach 91

The eighth position - Lower abdomen 92

The ninth position - Hands at the base of the neck 92

The tenth position - Arms at shoulder level 92

The eleventh position - Hands on the back 92

The twelfth position - Hands at the base of the spine 92

Additional positions First position 93

Second position 93

Third position... 93

Fourth position 93

Experiencing Presence - Treatment Session Conditions 93

Reiki exercises.. 95

Exercise 1... 96

Exercise 2... 96

Exercise 3... 96

Exercise 4... 97

Exercise 5... 97

Exercise 6... 98

Exercise 7... 98

Exercise 8... 99

Exercise 9... 99

Exercise 10.. 100

Exercise 11.. 100

Learn How to be Mindful During Energy Healing 101

Chapter 8 Practical Classes For You! 102

Gassho 102

Take a lotus or half lotus pose. 102

Reiji ho 103

Tiryo 105

Reiki Meditations 106

Muscle Tone Control 107

Breath Control 108

Emotion Control 110

Thought Flow Control 111

Breathing Techniques 113

Cleansing Breath 114

"Ha" - Breath 114

Breath for Clarifying Thinking 115

Calming Breath 116

Deep Breathing 116

Abdominal Breathing 117

Primal Breath (Fetal Breathing) 118

Full Breath 120

Directed Attention 121

Chapter 9 Unique Reiki Healing Practices 123

Kenyoku 125

Option One 126

Option Two 126

Option Three 126

Joshin Kokyu Ho 127

Activate energy centers. 127

Zakikiri Zoka Ho 128

Reiki Undo 129

Activate the three energy centers (Tribute). 129

Reiki Shower 131

Activate the three energy centers (Tribute). 131

Reiki Mawashi 131

Healing Practices 132

Beesen 135

Gyoshi ho 137

Affirmations 139

Activate the three energy centers. 139

Joshin Kokyu Ho 140

Activate the three Tributes. 141

Hishiryo 141

Activate the three energy centers. 141

Ge Doku Ho 142

Activate the three Tributes. 142

Hanshin Koketsu Ho 142

Activate the three energy centers. 142

Syu Chu Reiki 143

Activate the three energy centers. 143

Chapter 10 Yoga Therapy 145

Creating a Goal for the Whole Body 148

Creating a Goal for a Specific Organ 150

Optimal Background Tuning 151

Step two: optimize your lifestyle 152

Step three: work with the body 156

Chapter 11 Introduction to Meditation 166

A Timeline of Meditation Development & History 166

The Basics of Meditation 174

Preparing for Meditation 174

Basic Meditation Exercises 176

Mindfulness Meditation Exercise 176

Remedying Common Mistakes for Meditation Practice 179

Chapter 12 Introduction to Reiki 185

Health Benefits of Reiki 186

Reiki Healing for Anxiety & Stress 187

Anxiety 188

Common Symptoms of Anxiety 188

Causes of Anxiety Disorders 191

Chronic pain 191

Heart disease 191

Stress 192

Common Symptoms of Stress 192

Irritability 192

Depression 192

Difficulty breathing 193

Causes of Stress 193

Retirement 194

How Reiki Can Help 195

So Why 21 Days of Reiki? 196

Chapter 13 Introduction to Psychic Abilities 199

Connecting with your Intuition Again 202

Intuition Building Exercises 204

Set Challenges for Yourself 209

Get out of Your Comfort Zone 209

Walk in Other People's Shoes 210

Find your Kindred Spirits 212

Analyze your Thoughts and Beliefs 212

Keep a Curious Mind 214

Deepen Your Understanding 215

Become more Aware of the Details 215

Focus on your Emotions 217

Deepen Your Objectiveness.. 218

Listen to Inner Guidance 218

Pay Attention to Your Dreams 220

Write It Down 221

Psychic Skill Development 221

The Basics of Telekinesis 222

Exercises to Develop your Telekinesis.. 225

The Basics of Pyrokinesis... 228

Exercises to Develop your Pyrokinesis 230

Another practice you can work with is known as the Dancing Flame. 232

Aware and Mindful Breathing 237

Exercises to Develop your Empathy.. 239

The Basics of Astral Projection 239

Exercises to Develop your Astral Travel Skills.............................. 240

Another method that you can use is known as The Rope 241

The Risks and Benefits of Psychic Skills 242

Chapter 14 Root Chakra Reiki Meditation for Day One Through Three 247

Overview of the Mooladhara Chakra Root or 1st Chakra 247

Responsibilities of the Root Chakra 248

Day 1 Root Chakra Physical Meditation 250

Day 2 Root Chakra Mental Meditation 254

Chapter 15 Sacral Chakra Reiki Meditation Day Four Through Six............ 258

Overview of the Svadhisthana Chakra - Sacral or 2nd Chakra 258

Responsibilities of the Sacral Chakra 259

Imbalance Symptoms... 260

Day 4 Sacral Chakra Physical Meditation 262

Day 6 Sacral Chakra Spiritual Meditation 264

Chapter 16 Solar Plexus Chakra Reiki Meditation Day Seven Through 266

Nine 266

Overview of the Manipura Chakra - Solar Plexus or 3rd Chakra 266

Responsibilities of the Solar Plexus 267

Imbalance Symptoms 268

Day 7 Solar Plexus Chakra Physical Meditation 270

Day 8 Solar Plexus Chakra Mental Meditation 271

Day 9 Solar Plexus Chakra Spiritual Meditation 272

Chapter 17 Heart Chakra Reiki Meditation Day Ten Through Twelve 274

Overview of the Anahata Chakra - Heart or 4th Chakra 274

Responsibilities of the Heart Chakra 276

Imbalance Symptoms 276

Day 11 Heart Chakra Mental Meditation 278

Day 12 Heart Chakra Spiritual Meditation 279

Chapter 18 Throat Chakra Reiki Meditation Day Thirteen Through Fifteen 281

Overview of the Vishuddha Chakra - Throat or 5th Chakra 281

Responsibilities of the Throat Chakra 282

Imbalance Symptoms 283

Day 13 Throat Chakra Physical Meditation 284

Day 14 Throat Chakra Mental Meditation 285

Day 15 Throat Chakra Spiritual Meditation 286

Chapter 19 The Third Eye Reiki Meditation Day Sixteen Through Eighteen 288

Overview of the Ajna Chakra - Third Eye or 6th Chakra 288

Day 16 Third Eye Chakra Physical Meditation 292

Chapter 20 Crown Chakra Reiki Meditation Day Nineteen Through Twenty-

one 296

Overview of the Sahasrara Chakra - Crown or 7th Chakra 296

Responsibilities of the Crown Chakra 297

Imbalance Symptoms 298

Day 20 Crown Chakra Mental Meditation 301

Day 21 Crown Chakra Spiritual Meditation 302

Chapter 21 Daily Practical Tips 303

Center Yourself in Love and Truth 303

Do Not See the World in Black and White 305

Save Your Energy 306

Negative thinking 307

Conclusion 317

Introduction

Congratulations on downloading your copy of Chakra Meditation:

21 Days Guided Meditation to Awaken your Spiritual Power, Reduce Stress & Anxiety and Improve Awareness Psychic Abilities with Reiki Healing Exercises. My hope is that it includes everything that you are searching for on the subject of meditation, stress reduction and building your psychic abiltities as well as helpful information which you can start to apply to your life today to bring you a deep appreciation with your natural born gifts and how to use them.

In this comprehensive guide, you will out the history and basics or meditation, Reiki and several psychic abilities that we can all tap into. There is a wide range of exercises that you can perform to strengthen your intuition, your psychic abilities as well as meditation techniques to apply to your 21 day meditation which focuses on each chakra for three days.

The book goes further to give you guidance and clarity on the purpose and responsibilities of each chakra as well as which body parts that they are associated with. This will give you a better understanding about what chakra may be blocked if you having issues with the associated body parts. Knowing where the problems lie will help you to know what direction to go after the initial 21 day chakra meditation is complete.

You will also find out more of what symptoms are experienced on a physical and emotional level with each chakra and general advice in how to balance your chakras once again. You will then have a guided meditation for the duration of three days per chakra. Following the meditations and exercises are going to help each of your chakras to become balanced and energized.

There is also a chapter dedicated to how to keep your energy levels up during the day. Using protective and counter intuitive approaches, you will be able to keep others from taking your energy as well as it bleeding out of your system.

Once you have completed the book, you have knowledge in how to start healing your body from the inside out using the meditation techniques and exercises. There are plenty of books on Chakra Meditation, and thanks again for choosing this one! Every effort was made to ensure that it is full of as much useful information as possible.

Chapter 1 The Definition of Healing

What is Energy?

Energy, as you know now, is all around us. Every day we come into contact with Energy in space. It carries great potential for us, but unfortunately, only a few have opened up to realize its capabilities.

The Divine energy of the Universe can be used to maintain health, for spiritual growth, to feel joy from life, but unfortunately many only come to know their inner, powerful essence when there are so many problems that it is impossible to deal with them in the usual, traditional ways. The ways you knew and that you were used to.

But we came to this world in order to grow, improve, and there always comes a moment when you are faced with something new, with something that you never did and did not know. This begs the questions - what is healing? How can energy influence my healing and that of others?

Simply put, in one word - "Reiki."

What is healing energy, and how does it work?

Since energy healing surrounds the whole concept of Reiki, let me rephrase

-       what is Reiki? How does this work?

This name itself consists of two Japanese words - Ray and Ki. It is difficult to accurately translate them since Japanese words have many meanings: each word takes on a special meaning depending on the context. Since we are going to talk about spiritual healing, the word "Ray" we should probably translate as a divine spirit, wisdom permeating everything - both living and inanimate, and the word "Ki" - as non-physical energy that nourishes all living beings.

Universal wisdom (Ray) can be a source of guidance in our lives and help us improve. Energy (Ki) is present in all living things - in people, animals, and plants. A person filled with energy feels confident in his abilities. He is ready to enjoy life and overcome difficulties. With a lack of energy, a person loses strength and becomes more vulnerable, which is prone to the development of various diseases.

According to ancient Eastern philosophy, the Universe consists of Three Circles (Three Forces) - Heaven, Earth, and Man. The energy of Heaven's Ki (Heavenly Ki) always goes down, while the Earth's Ki always goes up. Human Ki is formed as a result of the collision of Heavenly and Earthly Ki. The human energy Ki created our world: minerals, plants, and living things.

It turns out that we experience the influence of Ki energy of two types - Heavenly and Earthly. Heavenly controls morality and Earthly desires, and understanding this system help balance these two types of influence. Thus, the concept of Reiki can be interpreted as non-physical healing energy, consisting of the energy of a life force controlled by a higher intellect (consciousness). So, at least, those who directly practice it determine the meaning of the Reiki technique. These people believe, or rather, feel that Reiki's energy is inherent in the intellect, which, in fact, directs it to where it is most needed. This energy creates in the body special healing conditions necessary for the individual development of the individual.

Do not confuse: it is about intelligence inherent in energy, and not about human intelligence in general. A person is not able to control this energy with the help of his mind, so it is not limited to his experience or abilities. Probably for the same reason, it cannot be used incorrectly or to the detriment. No, it always has a healing effect.

By the way, try to avoid one more mistake: do not confuse Reiki with the energy of a vital force, which can very well be radiated by the mind and create both favorable consequences and problems, including diseases. Here, we discuss positive energy.

The Energy Body

Let's talk in more detail about the energy of Ki. Where do we get it from? From the air, from food and water, from sunlight and sleep. And if she is not enough, we can help ourselves by using breathing exercises and meditation.

Ki is rightly considered a source of health. Passing through all organs and tissues, she revives them and supports them. It is clear that any violation of the flow of Ki is the main cause of the disease.

Interestingly, Ki is sensitive to thoughts and feelings. From the quality of thoughts and feelings, its flow intensifies or weakens. Negative thoughts and feelings can limit it, disrupt the healthy and harmonious flow of Ki.

By the way, Western doctors also admit that 98% of diseases are caused by our thoughts - directly or indirectly.

And if you think that thinking exists only in the brain, then you are mistaken. Like the nervous system, thinking permeates every organ and every tissue of our body. Moreover, it extends beyond the physical body and is located in a subtle energy field called the aura. The body and mind are closely connected, and only with their interaction is thinking created.

Now it becomes clear why negative thoughts, originating in the brain, gradually gather in various parts of the body and penetrate the aura. They block the flow of energy, preventing it from entering the tissues and organs as a result of which the latter begins to function worse. Our task is to remove negative thoughts and feelings, if, of course, we want to protect ourselves from illness.

But there is one problem. Yes, we can try to get rid of those thoughts and feelings that interfere with us and of which we ourselves are well aware. But what about the thoughts and feelings stored in the depths of the unconscious? How can we remove or change these thoughts and feelings, even if we are not aware of them?

This is where Reiki comes to our aid. Thanks to this method, we can unlock energy by working directly with the unconscious part of our brain. The Reiki stream, passing through a weakened or diseased area, as it wears out all negative thoughts and feelings. Sick organs and tissues again begin to receive a full supply of Ki energy. The energy balance in the body is restored, and disharmonious energies are supplanted.

The basis of Reiki, perhaps, should be considered our involvement in all of humanity. The idea that we are separated from the rest of the world is just an illusion. The wisdom we strive for is endless and accessible to all. Our task is to learn how to connect to the collective mind. How to do it? First of all, we must abandon the thought that we are all allowed. Thinking in this way, we contribute to the dispersal of the forces of goodness and love, and as a result, we feel lonely. Sometimes we do not want to consider ourselves part of a great whole for fear of losing personal freedom. This is wrong: we do not lose our freedom, combining it with a sense of integrity. Moreover, it is this combination, the ability to see in ourselves that which is one and the exclusive, which will allow us to find the right way to correct ourselves and the whole world.

Chapter 2 Energy Healing

The Reiki Story

None of the districts of Tokyo, there is the Saihoji Temple, next to which is a memorial dedicated to Mikao Usui, the creator of the Reiki method. The memorial was erected in 1927 by students of Mikao Usui, who founded the Reiki Society for the Treatment, a year after his death? This method is still popular today in Japan and in other countries.

The spiritual basis of the Reiki method was revealed by Mikao Usui during his three-week prayer and fasting on Mount Kurama, located north of the city of Kyoto, the former capital of Japan. Apparently, the very atmosphere of Kurama, covered with centuries-old trees, surrounded by pagodas and tall stuff all around, contributed to the emergence of the idea of sacred art associated with the spiritual healing of all diseases and the achievement of happiness.

The story of Reiki began in the mid-80s when Dr. Mikao Usui began to search for the ancient healing system, which, according to legend, was used by Christ and Buddha. Legend has it that this idea arose for a reason: his students moved the doctor to search. Having adopted Christianity, the Japanese scientist and philosopher became a priest, as well as the director of the Christian school for boys in Kyoto. The disciples, doubting the teacher's true faith, asked him to prove their faith in the Holy Scriptures in the same way as Jesus Christ did. In other words, they suggested that Usui perform one of the miracles that Jesus performed. The teacher could not do this, and then the students said that his faith was not enough to support faith in someone else.

Dr. Usui was so amazed at the depth of their approach to the issue of faith that he decided to immediately go to the West, where Christianity reigned. Mikao Usui was determined to learn how to perform miracles and, on his return, to demonstrate to his students' new evidence of his faith.

Mikao arrived in America, where he became a student at the University of Chicago. However, having deeply studied the Holy Scriptures of Christians, in particular, the description of miracles of healing, he realized that he could not put them into practice.

Nevertheless, giving up was not in the character of Mikao Usui: he began to study the sacred texts of other religions of the world. After ascertaining that the Buddha and his first disciples also performed miracles of healing, Dr. Usui carefully studied Buddhist manuscripts for seven years. He did not stop researching Buddhist sutras even when he returned home to Kyoto.

Mikao Usui tirelessly traveled around the country, visited temples and monasteries, talked everywhere with monks. From them, he learned that the Buddha did indeed often heal the sick, but this practice was lost by the Buddhists. The monks admitted that they focus mainly on their spiritual health, and consider physical healing to be the business of doctors. In short, Dr. Usui still could not find the answer to his question. Once, the abbot of a Zen Buddhist monastery invited him to live in a monastery to continue his research. After some time, Mikao Usui became a Zen Buddhist monk. After familiarizing himself with the sutras translated into Japanese, he began to study Chinese for a more accurate translation, since Buddhism penetrated Japan from China.

Then Dr. Usui began to study Sanskrit in order to read the sutras in the original. He found the required symbols but did not know at all what to do with them. It was then that Mikao Usui went to Mount Kurama, located a few kilometers from Kyoto, which the monks considered sacred.

For three weeks, Dr. Usui fasted and meditated in the expectation that he would reveal the meaning of mysterious symbols. He did not want to return to the monastery without receiving the right answer and even asked the rector to send monks for his remains if he did not return in 21 days.

As soon as he climbed the mountain, Dr. Usui piled 21 pebbles at the entrance to the cave, which became his shelter, and daily removed one of them so as not to lose track of time. Thus, 20 days passed, which Mikao Usui spent in a state of deep meditation, but nothing happened. And then came the last morning of the deadline set by him. In the dark predawn hour, Dr. Usui saw a sheaf of bright light directed directly at him. The first desire was to escape as far as possible from here, but Mikao Usui did not move. He suddenly realized that this was exactly the moment he had been waiting for so long. And if he once devoted himself to searching for many years, then he should not refuse to unravel the mystery even in the face of death. The experience was so strong that Dr. Usui lost consciousness.

When he came to consciousness, he suddenly realized he'd dreamed of "millions and millions of bubbles of all colors of the rainbow," and Reiki symbols loomed against the background of these bubbles. And not just symbols, because they were previously known to him: their meaning was revealed to him, and information was given on how to activate their healing abilities. This is how the first Reiki settings appeared in the modern world - the repeated and completely supernatural discovery of the ancient method of healing.

What do Energy Healers do?

Having made the discovery, Dr. Usui, the first energy healer, immediately went to Kyoto. He was in such a hurry that he stumbled and bruised his toe. Mikao Usui took this annoying incident as an opportunity to put his healing system into practice.

With a hand on his bruised finger, Dr. Usui took advantage of Reiki's energy and immediately felt that the pain had passed. This was the first proof of the truth of his discovery. Satisfied, he set off on. The path was not short, and after some time, Dr. Usui was very hungry. He went to the house by the side of the road and asked for food. The meal was taken out by the owner's granddaughter. Mikao Usui turned his attention to her swollen cheek. It turned out that the girl was tormented by severe toothache. But, as soon as he touched her cheek, the pain immediately disappeared, and the tumor began to subside right in front of their eyes. This was the second confirmation of his discovery, which led to the conclusion that Reiki can be used not only for self-medication but also for healing other people.

Returning to the monastery, Mikao Usui found the abbot completely sick. The unfortunate came down from a severe attack of arthritis. Needless to say, Mikao Usui immediately relieved him of pain and received another confirmation that the secret of the ancient healing art, which was used by all the great teachers, was revealed.

For the rest of his life, Dr. Usui practiced Reiki in Japan and taught others this art. The learning process was quite long: the students for a long time lived next to the master, learning Reiki. Dr. Usui considered training completed only when he was convinced that his students could put into practice everything that he himself knew about Reiki. Students gradually became masters themselves and went to society to heal people on their own. True, some followers of Dr. Usui, like the apostles of Christ, continued to live and work alongside their teacher.

Our Dynamic Multilayer Energy Field

For many centuries, healing work has been a mystery behind seven seals that defies any explanation. However, at present, some aspects of healing work can be explained from a scientific point of view. For example, the effectiveness of Reiki is explained by the theory of electromagnetic fields generated by all living things. This book is devoted to the book of Doctor of Philosophy James Oschman, "Energy Medicine, a scientific basis."

The presence of electric currents in the body has been known for a long time. One of the methods of self-regulation of the body are currents passing through the nervous system. The nervous system is associated with every organ, with every area of body tissue. It is through her that the brain sends its signals to regulate the activity of the body.

Another network through which electric current flows is the circulatory system. Blood passing through the blood vessels transmits "cardiac electricity" to every particle of our body.

Electric currents flow in each cell and between cells. Many of the cells actually contain liquid crystals. Living crystals are found in cell membranes, in the myelin sheaths of nerve fibers, and in many other places. All crystals have a piezoelectric effect, which manifests itself when exposed to pressure. Therefore, the liquid crystals of the body constantly generate an electric current. Currents are often coherent, which means that next to this area, there are always frequencies similar to those of the laser. These laser-like vibrations can propagate within the body and also radiate outward.

Scientific Studies That Prove That Energy Healing Works

Today, the studies of many foreign and American scientists have experimentally proved the existence of special energy-information processes that are fully consistent with Reiki's teachings on universal life energy.

Under the influence of research in this area, the point of view of Western scientists has changed. One of the reasons for this change was the invention of sensitive instruments to detect energy fields around the human body.

Subsequently, it was discovered that all tissues and organs produce certain magnetic pulsations, which became known as biomagnetic fields. Conventional electrical recordings, such as electrocardiograms and electroencephalograms, are now complemented by a biomagnetic recording called magneto cardiograms and magnetoencephalogram. For various reasons, mapping magnetic fields around the body often provide a more accurate definition of physiology and pathology than traditional electrical measurements.

Back in the 1920s, Harold Saxon Burr, an outstanding researcher who worked at the School of Medicine at Yale University, suggested that diseases could be detected in a person's energy field before their physical symptoms appear. In addition, Burr was convinced that diseases could be prevented by exposure to the energy field.

These concepts were ahead of their time, but are now validated in medical research laboratories around the world. Scientists use various instruments to determine how diseases alter the biomagnetic fields around the body. Others use pulsating magnetic fields to stimulate healing. Sensitive individuals have described these phenomena for a long time, but there was no logical explanation for how this could have happened.

In the early 80s, Dr. John Zimmerman, while conducting research at the University of Colorado in Denver, discovered that a strong biomagnetic pulsation emanated from a Reiki practitioner. The ripple frequency was unstable; it ranged from 0.3 to 30 Hz (cycles per second), most often in the range of 7–8 Hz. Biomagnetic pulsations emanating from the hands were in the same frequency range as his brain waves. Further scientific studies have shown that the entire frequency range has healing properties.

Confirmation of Zimmerman's research appeared in 1992 when Dr. Seto and his colleagues (Japan) began to directly examine masters practicing alternative healing methods. The energy emanating from their hands is so strong that it can be detected by a simple magnetometer, consisting of two coils with 80,000 revolutions of the wire. Subsequently, the experiments were expanded and transferred to sound, light, and thermal fields emitted by healers. The most interesting thing is that the ripple frequency changes all the time. Moreover, doctors investigating the therapeutic effects of pulsating magnetic fields have found that these frequencies are effective for healing both soft and hard tissues. Certain frequencies stimulate the growth of nerves, bones, skin, capillaries, and ligaments.

Reiki practitioners and their patients receive daily evidence of the effectiveness of this system (sometimes - even in hopeless cases!), and modern medicine is beginning to recognize this therapy as yielding results, which has been confirmed by new scientific studies.

Recently, research has been stepped up directly related to Reiki energy. During treatment, the internal and universal energies are combined in the hands of the practitioner, and this unity, regardless of philosophical, religious, or esoteric views, contributes to the healing process.

Scientists have conducted many experiments proving the effectiveness of the effects of Reiki energy at the cellular and other levels and even on inanimate objects. The objects of scientific research were unicellular organisms, plants, insects, laboratory animals, and such laboratory material as blood cells, neurons, cancer cells, water molecules, and, of course, the effect of energy on humans was studied in the most detailed way.

For example, the effect of Reiki energy on an open wound has been investigated. At the same time, two people were treated with the same damage to the skin, but one of them was exposed to the Reiki conductor hidden from him every day for 10 minutes. Doctors who observed the healing process also did not know about this effect. Four independent experts carried out monitoring measurements of the healing processes after five and ten days. The results were very different from each other. When a person was exposed to Reiki energy, the healing process went 50% after five days and 85% after ten. The second investigator stopped at the days of control measurements on the following results: 15% and 40%, respectively.

The presence of electric currents in the body has been known for a long time. One of the methods of self-regulation of the body are currents passing through the nervous system. The nervous system is connected with every organ, with every part of the body tissues, and it is through it that the brain sends its signals to regulate the activity of the body.

Another network through which electric current flows is the circulatory system. A saline solution of blood that travels over more than fifty thousand miles of blood vessels transmits "cardiac electricity" to every particle of our body.

The body has a secondary nervous system formed by perineurium, which is a layer of connective tissue surrounding each nerve. More than half of the brain cells are perineurium cells. Perineurium work on direct current. They control brain vibrations and are directly involved in the treatment process. If any part of the body is damaged, the perineural system generates an electrical potential in the damaged area, which puts the body in a state of readiness. Using these electrical potentials, the perineural system directs regenerative cells, such as white blood cells, fibroblasts, and motile skin cells, to the damaged area. When the treatment for the damaged area is completed, the electrical potential changes. The perineural system is also very sensitive to external magnetic fields.

When an electric current flows through a conductor, a magnetic field is created around it. The electric currents circulating in the human body generate magnetic fields, called biomagnetic, that permeate and surround the body. Sensitive magnetometers allow you to measure these biomagnetic fields. Dr. John Zimmerman of the University of Colorado College of Medicine, Denver, used a device called SQUID (superconducting quantum interference device) to measure biomagnetic fields in various parts of the human body, including the brain, heart, and many other organs. The measurements of the biomagnetic field made it possible to better understand how the body works and to improve the diagnosis of diseases.

The heart has the strongest biomagnetic field; it can be measured at a distance of 4-5 meters. The brain and all internal organs of the body are surrounded by their own biomagnetic fields. All fields have their own frequencies and interact with each other. When an organ is healthy, the frequency of its field is a well-defined quantity that changes if the organ's health is impaired. Adding together, all biomagnetic fields form a large aggregate biomagnetic field surrounding the body. This is very reminiscent of what we call an aura. Therefore, the biomagnetic field can be one of the main components of the aura, although other aspects are possible here.

Fields interact with other fields that are close to the body, including the fields of other people. The basis of this interaction is induction, that is, one magnetic field can affect another, as a result of which both the field itself and the strength and frequency of the currents passing through the conductor change. Thus, the biomagnetic field of one person affects the biomagnetic field of another person, which can affect the well-being of each of them, as well as the functioning of organs and body tissues. From this follows a completely definitive explanation of the concept of "magnetic personality." The same interaction of fields allows us to scientifically explain the therapeutic effect of one person on another.

So, from a scientific point of view, a human being does not end with skin, it extends beyond the physical body. We know this from personal experience, as we all sense the presence of other people. Now it has been proven and explained scientifically.

When Will Energy Healing Help Me?

Hands are also surrounded by a biomagnetic field - especially in people involved in healing. The healing energy of the hands, at least in part, is generated by the perineural system. This system surrounds nerve fibers, and it is through it that direct currents pass. Currents are modeled by vibrations emitted by the brain.

In addition to biomagnetic hands, other types of energy can also radiate, which also has a therapeutic effect. There is some evidence that infrared rays, microwave waves, and other types of photon radiation emanate from the hands of healers and that biological systems respond to them.

When a person is sick, the biomagnetic frequencies of some of his organs differ from their frequencies in a healthy state. Herbert Fröhlich, a researcher who discovered many interesting aspects in human biomagnetic fields, explains this process: "The association of cells forming a section of tissue or organs has a certain general frequency that regulates some important process, for example, cell division. Usually, these control frequencies are very stable. If for some reason, the cells change their frequency, the signals attracted from neighboring cells will tend to restore the correct frequency. However, if the frequency of a sufficiently large number of cells changes, the strength of the general vibrations of the system may decrease to the point where stability is lost. Loss of coherence leads to disorders and illnesses.

When the healer puts his hands next to the diseased organ and begins to heal it, the biomagnetic field emitted by his hands becomes much stronger than the field emitted by the diseased organ. In this case, the frequency of the biomagnetic field of the healer's hands approaches the frequencies that the diseased organ needs. Since the field of the healer is much stronger than the field of the diseased organ, it induces healthy frequencies in the field of this organ, forcing it to adjust its frequencies so that they again correspond to the healthy range. This regulation, in turn, affects the characteristics of electric currents flowing in the cells and the nervous system of the diseased organ and around it, as well as biological processes, as a result of which healing occurs.

The process can work in the opposite direction when the healer scans the patient's biomagnetic field or tries to find an area of disharmony in him. In this case, he slowly moves one or both hands at a distance of several centimeters from the body, paying attention to the sensations in his hands. The healer feels the changes radiated by the patient's field in the field of his hands. This allows him to determine where in the patient's biomagnetic field, there is an area with disturbed vibrations.

Hence, energy healing will help you to diagnose illness. Secondly, it will help you treat yourself and others. However, as you shall see, one of Reiki's unique qualities is its ability to come from tuning. The healer does not guide Reiki using his mind - the energy of Reiki itself finds the right direction.

Chapter 3 Levels of Energy Healing

Different Established Energy Healing Modalities

In Reiki, healing takes place on two levels - physical and spiritual. And it happens thanks to our connection with the very high spiritual vibrations of the Universe. This is precisely the secret of miraculous healing: the soul and body are healed not by human energy, but by the spiritual (vital) energy of the Universe. The healer passes it through himself while not spending his personal energy. The main task of the healer is not to bring his negative vibrations into Reiki's energy, to be as pure a conductor as possible. Only then can Reiki be used not only to cure diseases but also to achieve enlightenment and spiritual growth. When we ask Reiki for healing, we must be aware that help comes from the highest level.

The origins of the Japanese Reiki tradition can be found in the teachings of Yamabushi (holy hermits) on self-improvement, superpower, and the extension of life, dating back to the 7th century. Tradition always connected with the culture of the people, but one must understand that tradition and culture are not the same as spiritual teachings. The essence of spiritual teachings is to know the nature of man.

To practice Reiki, you do not need to become a Shinto or Buddhist. You just need to be able to incorporate this spiritual teaching into your own culture. In order to better understand the spirit of Reiki itself, it is very important to have an idea of the culture and traditions of Japan, but not be limited only to their external form. True spiritual values - spiritual growth, self-improvement, the ability to be oneself, and to reveal one's inner creative abilities, comprehension of one's own depths — are accessible to every person, regardless of the culture in which he is brought up.

From ancient times, the qualities known to people who embarked on the Path of spiritual growth have been known. The past masters are perfect, skillful mystics, insightful and mysterious, were too deep for their time.

The principles of Energy Healing

On the memorial plate, erected by students of Mikao Usui, the basic principles of Reiki are carved, which their teacher called to follow. As a matter of fact, these instructions were stated in poetic form by the Japanese emperor Mutsuhito, who made every effort to give his people a truly spiritual orientation.

The wise and subtle poetry of Emperor Mutsuhito was recited daily by members of the society created by Mikao Usui. The basic principles of Reiki became a guide in life, an inexhaustible food for the mind of those who grasped their deep meaning.

Agree, these are rather short, but very important instructions for development. After all, it was no coincidence that the ancient sages followed them, never ceasing to strive for self-improvement.

Mikao Usui believed that it was these principles that helped him to clearly and accurately formulate the purpose of his teachings, as well as to find the easiest and simplest ways to achieve this goal.

According to Mikao Usui, there is nothing complicated in mastering the Reiki method; everyone can master it. You just need to say the basic principles of Reiki every morning and every evening, sitting in a comfortable position and joining hands in prayer so you can develop a clean and healthy mind. This is, in fact, the essence of daily practice. Let's try to understand the principles of Reiki.

Let's start with the words that apply to each of them, and therefore by themselves become some kind of principles.

Being Connected to the Energy Field Awareness

The first words are, "Exactly today!" In fact, these words are the key to the secret of spiritual awakening. This key, which psychologists call "Here and Now," allows us to dissolve in the present and, breaking beyond the material world, get into the realm of love and light. This truth was revealed by Mikao Usui after 21 days of meditation and fasting on Mount Kurama.

Deep enlightenment, based on knowledge and experience accumulated throughout his life, allowed him to create a "System of Natural Healing" and transmit it to people. Thus, the main message of the mystical path of Reiki can be formulated as follows:

"Let your consciousness be here and now. This is the only way to come to the Great Divine Light. This is the only way to change your life for the better and give it a more spiritual meaning." The following principles are the other important steps to energy healing practice:

Principle 1 - Don't be Angry

You yourself know how often we are overcome by feelings such as anger, resentment, and hatred. Experiencing such emotions, we not only destroy ourselves but also cause irreparable harm to those around us. Where does so much hostility and annoyance come from?

Reiki meditative practices help us understand the true causes of negative emotions, get rid of them and harmonize our spiritual life.

Principle 2 - Do not Worry

The anxiety we experience affects us as destructively as anger. This state also has certain reasons, which meditation, contemplation, and intuition help to understand. With Reiki's help, we can translate basic energy, blocked by anxiety and fears, into constructive, meaningful actions.

Why are we even worried? It happens like this: one of the unconscious aspects of our senses ceases to control the important points necessary for survival. In other words, a sense of danger or threat is rooted in the subconscious. How to fix the situation is unknown. We cannot solve the problem, because we don't know what we are afraid of, and we begin to worry. However, in most cases, after realizing what is happening, the cause of fear turns out to be frivolous and easily eliminated.

The Reiki method is precisely able to free us from anxiety - both justified and completely far-fetched.

Principle 3 - Be Filled with Gratitude

How often do we forget about such a simple feeling as gratitude! But this is the energy of higher awareness, which exists only in man. Gratitude breeds trust and makes us part of a great whole. Forgetting gratitude, we seem to be losing ourselves. We leave unnoticed a helping hand extended to us by the Creator because we only strive for a specific kind of happiness and success. Thus, we deprive ourselves of all happiness and success. Showing gratitude, we recognize the greatness of creative power, its divine spark. So let us be attentive to any assistance provided to us, let us rejoice at everything that we receive.

It's not difficult to take this rule into your heart: you just need to understand that the right things always come to us at the right time, and not demand more.

Principle 4 - Work Hard

Performing any work, you need to try to maintain a meditative state of mind, completely immerse yourself in the workflow precisely "here and now." This, perhaps, will be the best application of accumulated spirituality in real life.

Principle 5 - Be Kind to Others

Imbued with love for other people, that is, to recognize and honor the Divine in them, is not an easy task. To make it easier, you need to try to feel yourself a part of the Universe, a part of the great whole. This does not detract from personal freedom. On the contrary, only a combination of freedom and involvement in the common allows us to gain the strength of goodness and love. Anyone who is not capable of this is doomed to loneliness.

Primary Awareness Exercise

As you can see, the life principles of the "System of Natural Healing" by Mikao Usui is not a strict set of rules that must be strictly observed; it is rather a call to more carefully examine your own behavior and try to get rid of senseless habits. These principles make us think once more about our own lives. They can also be perceived as some spiritual riddles mobilizing our rational mind, used to control everything to the smallest detail, to learn something new in life. Finally, mastering these principles can significantly help in a practical approach to the Reiki method.

Energy Healing Practices

Reiki practices can change a person's life and teach him a lot. They allow you to better know yourself, make life joyful, and happy.

Reiki is a system of natural healing. It is very simple - this, perhaps, is its secret. To many, this seems strange - after all, we are used to living by the principle: "The more difficult, the better the result." Overcoming obstacles instill a fighting spirit in us, arouses interest, provides food for the mind, and satisfies our Ego.

However, what is attractive to the Ego does not lead to spiritual growth, and a simple technique can give real growth. So, choose for yourself what is more important and more valuable for you.

Meditation

Osho Meditation is a system of meditative techniques. She is not called to teach or give anything. It grows from within, from your wholeness. This is observation, or rather, the quality of observation, the quality of a conscious, alert state, a state of no-mind. This is the joy of life, affirming, and causeless. The constant dying for the past and the birth of a new quality of being, openness to this new. And the technique itself is just a way to create the right conditions for a positive energy flow.

Who is Osho, and why has Osho meditation become known all over the world? Osho (Bhagwan Sri Rajneesh) was a spiritual leader and mystic; he was born and raised in India. Osho created a system that combines religion and philosophy, and involved followers in it.

Osho Philosophy

There is a misconception that meditation is a way to come to harmony and change what you don't like. Beginners think that the problems will disappear, and silence will reign in the head.

Osho proposed a new approach. He believes that meditation does not need a goal. To eternally hurrying residents of megalopolises, it seems that everything that has no purpose is a waste of time.

Everything that we should gradually wean from gives the philosophy of Osho meditation. No race for results, exhausting goals, and the opportunity to practice without preparation. A space free of obligations, apart from the main thing, is to enjoy the practice.

Since emotions and the mind live in the physical body, you need to start first with this. Subtle matters can be started when the body is ready and open to practice.

Imagine a three-year-old child who seriously expects to pick up a bag of potatoes. He is not physically ready for such a load. Also, working with the inner subtle plans is the next level of growing up. To begin with, let's take care of our own body, nourish it with our forces and let it be understood that we remember about it.

The essence of Osho's meditations is to allow energy to flow freely throughout the body. If you are already tensed by reading the word "energy," then I hasten to reassure you - energy is a force that is born at the junction of calm and relaxation. When you start the practice, you will feel how this energy washes away, like water, the husks of fuss and habitual anxiety. Imagine the crabs that the wave washed ashore. The next wave will take the animals back to the ocean and wash their tracks. Also, the practice of meditation helps restore inner purity and silence.

Osho practices begin with the active part because it is familiar to the mind. The mind is unlikely to resist if you are dancing or running. At the active stage, we release anxiety and suppressed emotions, prepare the mind for practice.

The active stage can be different - dance, laughter, running, breathing. The most unusual technique is gibberish. During this practice, you release your body on all sides and do whatever you want. Angry - stamp your feet, clench your fists and scream. Sad - hug yourself, cry, stand motionless. Rejoice - laugh, jump. You can do literally anything. The main thing is to give vent to emotions through the body, let go of yourself and throw out everything.

Next to the active stage is the stage of silence. The more emotions you release in the first part, the quieter and deeper the second part of the practice will turn out.

What meditation should a beginner choose?

Osho developed one hundred and twelve methods of meditation. I recommend that beginners learn two basic meditations - Dynamic and Kundalini. With experience, proceed with the rest of the methods. I discuss these in the chapter "Reiki Meditations."

The main morning technique is Osho Dynamic Meditation. It relaxes the body and gives it strength for the coming day. Meditation lasts an hour and consists of five stages: chaotic breathing, thoughtless movements, jumping with arms raised, complete stillness and silence, and spontaneous flowing dance. For beginners, we recommend that you go to a quiet spot and master the techniques.

Evening Meditation - Kundalini Meditation. It helps to digest what happened during the day, relax the body, and release control. Meditation consists of erratic body shaking, smooth dance and complete immobility. Each previous stage releases even more energy, calming the body and mind.

For beginners to meditate, we suggest choosing for yourself the methods by which you will meditate in the morning and evening. It is better to invest your forces gradually, without immediately embracing 112 methods.

Awakening the Body Response

Imagine you are walking along an empty street and towards you - a cat. You see a cat, and at that moment, an observer wakes up in you. Then your internal observer steps aside and sees both you and the cat on an empty street. The essence of meditation is to separate the inner observer from the physical body and look at the sides. The bonus of this approach is that you can practice anywhere. Walking down the street, talking with colleagues, reading a book. After some time, you will be able to take a neutral position. The next stage of practice is to learn to observe your emotions and mood.

Osho teaches us to watch constantly. If we practice only an hour a day, sitting still in meditation, then for the remaining twenty-three hours, we will do exactly the opposite.

To watch is to look in the inner mirror. When you observe your thoughts and acknowledge the existence of everything that happens, an extraordinary silence sets in. There is no one to argue with. No one is attacking, so no need to defend. Saying "I'm angry" to ourselves and stepping back two steps to the side, we give ourselves the opportunity to feel the situation without experiencing toxic guilt for the "wrong" emotion. There is no internal censor who decides which emotions are good and which are bad. Then the energy of observation returns and gives all the accumulated power to you. Like natural elements.

What to remember: In the Osho tradition, there is no term "novice." You can practice without preparation. Practice does not require special equipment, and you can perform it at any time of the day. Although it is accepted that the best time to practice is dawn or dusk.

The main rule of Osho - let meditation bring pleasure and joy. Practicing for pleasure does not mean that on difficult days, you need to give up everything, though. Remember to practice every day and meditate no matter the circumstances.

Deep Touch

Deep Touch is a practice that harmoniously combines work with the body, energy, and attention. It would seem that we all know how to walk, sit, lie down, and get up. But are we doing it right? Admittedly, no.

Due to improper walking, we lose a huge amount of energy and gain health problems, especially with the spine. But our body is the only thing that indisputably belongs only to us. Only through the body do we work with our consciousness.

Deep Wave

All surrounding space, the whole world is riddled with waves. Of course, we don't even notice it. This state of affairs is so usual and familiar to us that we simply do not pay attention to it. Meanwhile, the waves penetrate everything, often without colliding with anything and without stopping at anything.

In the practice of the Deep Wave, technology has been developed that allows us to create an environment in our physical body that can catch the subtlest vibrations and in which their energy can settle.

Deep Sound

In the world around us, everything sounds without exception, including man. However, far from everyone knows how to sound competently. The practice of Deep Sound allows you to learn to tune the body so that it becomes a high-quality sound resonator, and use certain forms of internal attention. This effective technology of working with yourself and with your voice leads to real growth - the emergence of Deep Sound.

Deep Gymnastics

Also referred to as yoga, this is another way to work individually with your body. The difference from ordinary gymnastics, at first glance, is very small: a slower movement and a different focus of attention - not on an external object, but inside your being. But no wonder they say that everything ingenious is simple. The technique gives an amazing effect. It has a general healing effect on the whole body - thanks to it, not only the quality of muscles and tendons improves, but also a feeling of holistic perception of oneself arises.

Chapter 4 Energy Healing Initiation and Steps

Today, there are a large number of different areas of Energy Healing. Some of them are called traditional, some - non- traditional. One of the traditional destinations is Reiki Usui Shiki

Ryoho.

It should be noted that the Reiki tradition in the form in which it is now, did not arise immediately. It was formed, changed, and developed. Actually, it continues to develop today. Such is the natural property of a living tradition

-      the desire to develop in changing living conditions. At the same time, there is something unchanging - the basis without which tradition would cease to exist.

In Reiki Usui, Shiki Ryoho, this form is defined by nine elements and four aspects. Thanks to their existence, it is possible to transmit the mystery that Reiki is.

What is a tradition for? Primarily for security. In Reiki Usui, Shiki Ryoho, this security is realized in a natural way - in all the actions prescribed by tradition. Reiki is transmitted through initiation, and at the same time, can be transferred to any person. And as a result, a person receives what he now most needs, what is most capable of supporting his life. The second important role of tradition is that it gives a person the opportunity to do with ourselves, and sometimes with another person, something that in ordinary life we never do. More precisely, it gives permission for this. What a person does is not that he just suddenly wanted to, but that which is sanctioned by the subtle world. This sanction in Reiki was given to Mikao Usui (remember - on Mount Kurama?).

The third merit of tradition is that it gives a feeling of reliability. The fact that Reiki Usui Shiki Ryoho is already about 100 years old and over the years hundreds of thousands of people have studied this practice (or maybe more) is a definite test of time.

When a person regularly practices Reiki Usui Shiki Ryoho, then he really gets the best and necessary for his life. And even if he does not always immediately understand this, tradition does its job. It honestly fulfills its role, providing primarily efficiency, reliability, and safety.

The elements and aspects that describe the Reiki tradition of Usui Shiki Ryoho did not arise immediately - not from the first years of Reiki's existence. However, knowing them will allow us to understand a little better what we get from Reiki and how best to transmit it to other people.

Listed below are the elements and aspects of Reiki Usui Shiki Ryoho:

1. The mystical order

2. The technique of healing

3. Spiritual discipline

4. Personal growth

Mikao Usui, in his book "Usui Reiki Ryoho Hikkei" wrote: "From time immemorial, it often happened that one who comprehended the ancient secret teaching, either kept it for himself or shared it only with his heirs. This secret was not passed on to any of the outsiders. However, this tradition of the last century has already gone out of fashion. In our time, the happiness of mankind is based on the joint work of people and their desire for social progress. That is why I will never allow a single person to possess this knowledge only for themself. Our Reiki healing is a completely original method, and it cannot be compared with any other method in the world. That is why I would like to make this method available to the people for the prosperity of all mankind. Each of us has the potential to receive a divine gift, which leads to the unification of the soul and body. Through Reiki, a great many people can feel a divine blessing. Our Reiki healing is an original therapy that builds on the spiritual   energy of   the universe. Through it, a person first gains health, and then a calm mind, and joy in life will increase. Today we need to improve and rebuild our lives so that we can free our loved ones from illness and emotional suffering. This is the reason why I dared to freely teach people this method.

Today we need to improve and rebuild our lives so that we can free our loved ones from illness and emotional suffering. This is the reason why I dared to freely teach people this method."

You are about to learn all about it...

Initiation

Initiation is an ancient way of transferring energy and sacred knowledge from one person to another. This method has long been used by spiritual teachers and masters of the whole world in cases where energy or knowledge cannot be transmitted through words.

In almost all spiritual traditions, symbols and mantras are used for meditation, working with energy, healing, and personal development. Some of them are capable of causing subjective changes; others are objective. Symbols and mantras include symbolically significant objects (cross, Yin and Yang symbols, light, various shapes, and colors). With their help, certain moods and associations are created.

For energy healing, this consists of Reiki symbols and mantras, runes, and magical amulets. In order to work with them, it is necessary to receive instructions from someone who has already dealt with them and is capable of initiating, that is, transferring the energies acting in them. If we cannot receive such instructions, or simply want to achieve the goal with our own efforts, we must first spiritually set ourselves up for the corresponding system of symbols and learn how to use them correctly.

You can, for example, turn to Tantric Buddhism - the spiritual path from which Reiki arose. Here, the exact rituals and recitation of mantras during favorable astrological periods are connected with the sequence of visualizations of the mantras and the evocation of a certain deity in a state of deep meditation.

It is these opportunities that Mikao Usui used on Mount Kurama. He managed to establish a connection with the spiritual traditions behind the symbols and mantras. He gained the ability to connect with Reiki energy and began to use symbols and mantras for subsequent initiation.

However, we have already said that Kurama is known as a place especially favorable for meditation and spiritual practices. And since not everyone is able to be there, it becomes obvious that initiation, that is, the transfer of human knowledge to man, is a simpler, more accessible, and less demanding path.

First, you need to understand that symbols and mantras are not Reiki yet. They can only be used within the Reiki system after traditional initiation. Otherwise, they will remain signs and words, no different from any others. Even with Mikao Usui, the symbols and mantras found by him in Sanskrit manuscripts made no impression until he made a certain spiritual setting.

We must also understand that relying on the power and influence of symbols and related mantras within Reiki is possible only if used correctly. Only after receiving personal initiation, symbols, and mantras from simple hieroglyphs turn into an accurate and powerful tool for working with energy.

Steps

The traditional Reiki system has always consisted of three levels - Shoden (entry), Okuden (immersion), and Shinpiden (sacrament). Today, the fourth step has also been added to them - the Workshop, aimed at "teacher training."

As a result of initiation at each of these steps, the student receives "settings" for Reiki energy, theoretical knowledge and learns meditative and healing practices.

At whatever stage of Reiki comprehension, you may be, you should know some rules:

-       Reiki method can be used simultaneously with other methods of treatment.

-       The more you practice Reiki treatment, the more powerful and sophisticated it becomes.

-       You should not complicate Reiki too much.

-       Reiki can be used in everyday life. This method should become part of your existence, and then you can apply it in any situation.

-       Reiki can help even in one minute with just a touch or a close look.

-       Treatment should only be given to those who wish to receive it.

-       Using the Reiki method, you can heal yourself, other people, animals, plants, energize any objects, including stones and amulets, purify energy and fill it with rooms, food, and drink.

-      One of the important conditions for healing is the purity of intent.

The Reiki stepped system allows you to calmly and smoothly climb to the top at an individual pace. To improve healing abilities, of course, constant practice is necessary.

The first step

Shoden (entry) - understanding the basics of the spiritual method of healing Reiki.

-      "Settings" on Reiki energy.

-      An explanation of the Reiki method.

-      Basic meditative and healing practices.

-      Hand positions during healing.

At the first stage, you learn to work with energy, to feel its flow. The healer's experience is gaining - how the energy goes, what resonance is felt in the hands when healing a person, animal, plant, inanimate object; how quickly it is possible to calm thoughts, emotions during meditation, the depth of immersion in oneself.

This is a kind of preparation for the transition to the second stage, in which treatment occurs not only through the hands, through touching the object of healing, but mentally, at the level of awareness and intention. By regularly performing meditative and healing practices, you heal the mind and body, emotional state, purify and harmonize the energy flows in the body and prepare yourself for a new, higher level of work with Reiki energy.

The second step

Okuden (immersion) - an increase in the strength of Reiki and the expansion of the possibilities of using Reiki.

-       Settings for three Reiki characters.

-       Theory: remote treatment; the study of symbols (their origin, purpose, and practical application).

At the second stage, you learn to transmit healing energy in time and space; use Reiki symbols to transfer energy to any distance (into the past, present and future); to heal not only people, animals, objects, but also situations, relationships with other people; You can also protect yourself, objects; heal habits, behavior; work with emotions; successfully implement a plan and so on.

In the second stage, you learn to work more deeply with yourself and with other people. People begin to become more aware of the processes that happen to them and their loved ones, to work more consciously with the healing energy of Reiki.

The third step

Shinpiden (sacrament) - further spiritual growth, increased intuition, healing abilities.

-       Setting for the fourth Reiki character.

-       Theory: on the origin, meaning, and practical application of the symbols.

-       The technique of energy amplification - Reiju.

In the third stage, further spiritual growth occurs. After the student has gained enough experience in distance treatment, in meditative practices, learned to better control his thoughts, emotions and much more, he is ready to move on to the third level of training, that is, to an even higher level of energy work. At this level, the ability to heal and self-clean with Reiki is markedly increased.

The third step is the threshold of the Workshop. Not everyone feels the desire or willingness to devote themselves to the work of the Master. After all, this is a completely different level of work with energy, a great responsibility to students, high requirements for personal qualities.

In the Japanese tradition, you can go through the third step and continue your spiritual growth by taking the fourth, very powerful symbol for personal spiritual growth - a symbol of spiritual enlightenment. Indeed, many people turn to Reiki in order to learn how to treat themselves, their friends and relatives, to learn how to meditate, to control themselves in difficult situations, to purify themselves from negative energies, to cultivate oneself spiritually, to recognize the causes of failures and ailments, to successfully solve life problems, to learn the laws of the Universe etc.

And advancement to the third step allows them to more effectively and successfully improve in this.

The fourth step

The level of the Master (Teacher) is the level that gives the right to teach others the Reiki method.

First, you need to go through the initiation to the level of the Reiki Master (Teacher). Only then can one gain the right to initiate at the first stage of Reiki and begin to gain relevant experience.

In parallel with this practice, training takes the form of classes in which you study:

-       make settings for the second, third and workshop stages;

-       conduct a theoretical course of each step;

-       conduct meditative and healing practices in a group.

As already mentioned, the level of the Master (Teacher) is an even higher level of work with energy. You re-comprehend the essence of the first, second, third, and Workshop of Reiki steps. In addition to owning theoretical and practical teaching material, the Master should be able to control himself, constantly improve, and be able to help students on their spiritual Path. No wonder they say that there is no better way to learn something than by starting to teach it. Each initiation or lesson you take in a group opens up new possibilities for understanding the Reiki method and energy. And there is no limit to this perfection.

Circle Training

One of the conditions for receiving initiation is compulsory training. The training takes place on the Reiki circle, conducted by the Master. During the training, skills are transferred on how to use what was received during the initiation. The master also answers the student's questions.

During training, the first step is passed on how to do a Reiki session for yourself and another person. Learning takes the form of oral transmission. At the same time, it is clearly stipulated that the training takes place (first stage, second stage, third stage). A certain amount of information and a "key" are transmitted, allowing you to use it correctly.

Oral Tradition

Reiki is an oral tradition. What is written in the book is just information, not a Reiki broadcast. Reiki practice is transmitted by the Master personally to the student, in person. Information can be distributed widely and accessible to everyone. And the sacrament can only be transmitted to a person personally.

With oral transmission, in addition to information, something else is transmitted that cannot be transmitted without personal contact. The story of Reiki is a story about people's lives, thanks to which we now have the opportunity to learn this practice and practice it. In Reiki sessions, both the narrator and the listeners live some of their internal events. And this residence gives an invaluable experience of touching the mystery of what happened in the mind of Mikao Usui when he went to get Reiki. And then to pass it on to people.

Each of us goes his own life; each carries out his search and makes his own choice. The example of Mikao Usui allows us to decide for ourselves what to do in similar situations. And history gives a chance to feel, catch what Mikao Usui relied on when the people around him were ready to accept his gift. And if he had not achieved this, Reiki would not have reached us. But he managed to achieve this by doing a great job not only outside, but also inside himself.

Reiki Symbols

There are four characters in Reiki Usui Shiki Ryoho. These symbols are not a secret - they are passed on to everyone who receives the second stage. But at the same time, they are a mystery; that is, they not only have an external form but are also endowed with something more.

We will not give an image of these symbols here, since these are just drawings, and their essence, filling through a book cannot be transmitted. If you decide to do Reiki, then you will be introduced to them by the Master - the person who will teach you. And then you yourself will begin to build your relationship with symbols and with Reiki through symbols.

Here is a quote from the book of the Japanese Master Reiki, a member of the Usui Reiki Ryoho Gakkai (Tokyo) society, Mr. Hiroshi Doi, "The Modern Method of Reiki Healing": "The symbols presented in Reiki for working with higher energy techniques are easily applicable. In the Japanese Reiki tradition, symbols are not given as much importance as in the Western tradition, where the number of symbols is increasing.

In the Japanese tradition, the role of Reiki symbols is exactly the same as the supporting wheels of a bicycle when you learn to ride. Anyone can ride a bike with support wheels. The shape of the support wheels can be different as long as the "support" function is satisfied. The same can be said of Reiki symbols.

Symbols facilitate the use of Reiki energy. The symbols are useful, convenient, and enjoyable to use, but Reiki healers should leave them when they have grown enough as healers (supporting wheels are also removed when a person has learned to ride a bicycle well). Symbols need to be used as a tool. You should not have a misunderstanding of the function of symbols. It's pointless to look for new additional characters or consider them sacred.

Usui-sensei did not use symbols but said: "Use symbols well. Use them more and more, and you will find yourself at a level where you no longer need symbols. The human mind can instantly reach anywhere in the universe. You need to grow so high that you no longer need symbols."

In other spiritual practices, symbols are mostly of religious significance or given as a revelation for spiritual growth. But the symbols used in Reiki do not have that meaning. They are designed to facilitate the implementation of higher Reiki techniques with the help of vibrations and resonance characteristics of symbols.

When using characters, two effects occur:

-       The shape of the characters has its own vibration, the resonance of which can be used.

-       Mental energy vibration occurs when you understand the action of a symbol. Then there is a resonance between your energy and the energy of the symbol.

First, the first effect occurs, and then you can get the second. When you learn to control the energy of your mind, you can no longer use symbols.

You should study all the characters and learn how to use them correctly. Then you will need to achieve a level of non-use of characters. You decide when to use the first three characters, and then the fourth character. After that, you will understand that you are ready to rise above the symbols.

If you have any doubts or misconceptions or you do not feel any effect from moving to the next stage, you can use all the symbols as before. If you practice long and long enough, you are so filled with Light that one day, you yourself become a symbol of Light. But it is you who decide (feel) when to make this transition.

So, in the second stage of Reiki, you apply three characters. At this stage, the flow of Reiki energy for healing doubles compared to the first stage, you become able to better use Reiki energy in various ways.

1st character

The meaning is to heal and purify at the level of matter and body. The first symbol is called the symbol of increasing power and can be used in various ways since it contains a higher power. It is used alone or with other symbols

-    to increase their strength. It may also have protective value.

2nd character

The meaning is to heal and purify at the level of spirituality and the subconscious. The second symbol is a symbol of love and harmony. It is sophisticated and full of harmony. A distinctive feature is that it sends the energy of balance and harmony precisely to an object that does not have a form, for example, to feelings. Harmonizes the emotional and mental energies. It is used both independently and together with the first character.

3rd character

The meaning is to heal and purify from a distance, in the past, present, and future. This symbol is a conductor in space and time. It helps transfer energy from a distance. It is effective when used together with the first and / or second character. Directs energy directly to the center of the essence, located outside of time and space - this is its distinctive feature. It is mainly used for healing at a distance, cleansing karma and injuries, and for creating a beautiful future.

4th character

In the third stage of Reiki, one symbol is used, which replaces all previous ones.

Chapter 5 Learning to Read the Energy Field

The main practice in Reiki Usui Shiki Ryoho is a Reiki session. You can do a Reiki session for yourself or another person, or you can get it from another person. Anyone conducting a Reiki session must have Reiki initiation and undergo training.

During the session, open palms are placed on the human body. This is done by the one who is conducting the session. He does nothing else. He only puts his palms, and Reiki does the rest.

Each person feels the session differently, and each one receives something of their own in the session. That which is most necessary for him at a given moment in time. That which has his inner consent.

Thanks to Reiki sessions, even quite serious illnesses are sometimes cured, a life situation or a person's attitude to it changes. However, there a few things you must learn. That is what this chapter of this book is dedicated to.

Increase Positive Energy and Avoid the Negative Energy

With the help of Reiki, we can cleanse, heal, and harmonize the energy centers - chakras. Agreeably, we are often overreacting to difficult life situations. No matter what we feel - anger, fear or aggression, we feel at this moment completely unprotected. At the same time, we don't even realize that we ourselves are the source of such sensations. External life only provokes us to manifest our inner imbalance.

The situation can be corrected by learning to be distracted from external problems and concentrate on internal energy - the energy of the chakras. After all, it is her imbalance that is the cause of the violation of our internal balance.

Energy movement and the Chakra

In order to heal with the help of Reiki the seven main chakras, it is necessary to know their location, and the properties of the energy flow passing through them. Then you can meditate with each of the chakras until you reach a feeling of complete balance.

Unlocking and Balancing the Chakras

Unlocking the chakras is to determine the causes of the blocks and the malfunctioning of energy centers, and their subsequent elimination. However, preventing the blocking of energy nodes is much easier than working with closed chakras. Unlocking energy centers requires determining the causes of blocks for each energy center.

- Fear is the cause of the Muladhara blocks.

- The second energy center of Swadhisthana is destroyed by guilt.

- The center of self-realization of Manipura is exposed to the emergence of blocks as a result of shame.

- Grief is the cause of the destruction of the Anahata love center.

- Lies, including to oneself, block the Vishuddha chakra.

- Unlocking is necessary for the center of intuition of Ajna if a person lives in a world of illusions.

- The divine center of the Sahasrara is destroyed by strong earthly attachments.

When energy is Unbalanced or Blocked?

Is it possible to unlock the chakras yourself, you may ask? Self-unlocking of the chakras is possible as much as a person's desire. Working with the energy system requires a serious and responsible approach. One-time meditations and periodic visits to yoga centers are not sufficient efforts. Unlocking the chakras in a person is a rather painstaking work that requires daily exercise.

Meditative practices help but also involve difficult work with one's own mind. The results may not come very soon, which, of course, often deprives enthusiasm. Yogic asanas aimed at activating certain chakras may seem too difficult for beginners to perform physically. The development of the body, as well as the improvement of the energy system, does not tolerate haste. Unlocking the chakras on your own will require your self-control and seriousness.

How can chakras be unlocked on the human body? Before you unlock the chakras, you need to find out the cause of the blocks. As we have already found out, each energy center has its own reason for blocking. Therefore, each energy node requires a specific approach to unlock.

- Chakra Muladhara is destroyed by fears. To cope with them, they need to meet, look at them, and feel.

- Guilt blocking Swadhisthana is subjected to the same method. Feelings of guilt must be analyzed, accepting the real reasons for it and removing the illusory.

- The same applies to shame that destroys Manipura.

- Unlocking the Anahata chakra, blocked by sorrow, requires a lot of willpower and sometimes time.

- Working with Vishuddha has a basic rule - do not lie. Speaking a lie to others, we begin to do the same in dialogs with ourselves. This blocks the speech center.

- Ajna opens and closes blocks if reality is added to his perception of the world.

- The Sahasrara is cleansed by letting go of earthly attachments.

Is there a universal practice for unlocking chakras?

As I already mentioned, unlocking the chakras requires a serious and high- quality approach, including working with each energy center. The best practice is to unlock the chakras in turn. The universal technique is the practice of working with the middle Anahata chakra. The heart center connects the lower chakras with the upper. Charging this energy center, we supply energy and open all the others. Again, this technique of unlocking the chakras is not sufficient. Despite its versatility, it requires additional work with each energy center.

First Chakra

The first chakra - Muladhara (root) - is located at the base of the spine. It is the source of our existence because it closely connects our body with the Earth. The first chakra is responsible for our survival - for food, clothing, shelter, protection, and procreation.

The first sign of imbalance in the first chakra is a sense of danger.

Go for a walk just to mingle with nature. Take a closer look at the life boiling around you. Feel how it is imbued with life force. Nature fills everything that exists with life - trees and grass, animals and birds, rivers, and mountains. Her power pervades you, feel it. Realize that you are not living life, but life is living by you. Understand that there is a force that gives you life, makes your heart beat, your lungs breathe, and blood runs through your veins. Recognize yourself as part of nature, and a sense of fear will leave you.

Second Chakra

The second chakra - Swadhisthana - is located in the pelvic area. Its main driving force is the search for pleasure. The main desire is a sensual and sexual activity, the desire to plunge into the ocean of sensations, to feel attractive and to be able to get whatever you want.

With the unbalanced second chakra, the pursuit of pleasure never ends with a sense of pleasure. Remember the feeling of satisfaction that made you feel guilty. Restore the object of pleasure in your memory and try again to experience all the sensations, but this time fully aware of them. Describe your feelings. Did this experience bring you pleasure? In what place of your body are the experienced sensations concentrated? Realize them fully. Surely you will find that your ability to enjoy has become much wider. Now it's much easier for you to achieve it.

Third Chakra

The third chakra - Manipura - is located in the solar plexus. It is a source of self-confidence, self-awareness. Thanks to her, we are able to distance ourselves from the influence of the outside world and at the same time, exert influence on it.

The main signs of instability of the third chakra are guilt that embraces us when someone refuses something, fawning over others, a constant sense of ourselves as a victim, a feeling of helplessness and an inability to fend for ourselves. Once in a conflict situation, we can balance the third chakra by asking ourselves two very important questions.

1.   Is something really threatening me? (Is my safety or even survival in jeopardy?)

2.   Do I really care about the outcome? (If I win the fight, will it mean something to me?)

Fourth Chakra

The fourth chakra - Anahata - is located in the region of the heart.

The "path of the heart" is not a life strategy, but joy in all its manifestations. It allows you to live your life and influence the material world.

The main manifestation of the unbalanced fourth chakra is sentimentality. When our heart is broken, we are not able to separate our problems from those of others. The imbalance of the fourth chakra is also manifested in an exaggerated immersion in love and dependence. Learn to listen to your heart, and soon it will become a habit with you! You will gain a sense of comprehensive calm. Accept with gratitude what people want to give you. Let them feel the joy of doing a good deed.

Fifth Chakra

The fifth chakra - Vishudha - is located in the neck. Having opened it, we begin to perceive our own giftedness, no matter what manifests itself. The main property of the fifth chakra is the awakening of your inner voice, capable of telling you the truth.

With the unbalanced fifth chakra, we realize our right to independent thinking, but we cannot put its manifestation in order. We are in a constant struggle for personal freedom.

Analyze everything you believed in before. What were your ideas about life? After all, it was this which influenced your life. It was this which shaped your point of view. Try to consciously change and expand your range of beliefs; this will give a powerful impetus to your discovery of your uniqueness.

Concentrate on your breathing, as it is through it that energy comes to you. Focus on the depth of breathing; try to make it even deeper and slower. You will feel that your anxiety disappears. You are immersed in a state of peace and tranquility.

Sixth Chakra

The sixth chakra - Ajna - is located in the forehead, at the point between the eyebrows. The ultimate goal of the sixth chakra is inspiration and grace. This is a world of images that arise in our thoughts. However, she also has the opposite extreme - the desire to escape from reality into the world of illusions.

The unbalanced sixth chakra allows fear to completely absorb our personality. But if we realize that we are in an unbalanced state, if we can look inside ourselves and find the source of this fear, then we are able to overcome it.

Try to answer the following questions:

- What are you dreaming about?

- What is your imagination striving for?

- What images dominate your fantasies?

- Do you seek to plunge deeper into the world of fantasy, or is the mind overpowering your imagination?

Become a witness to your own life. This will mean that you have taken the first step towards the development of the spiritual will. Describe your feelings and try to understand in which direction your imagination is moving - healthy or pathological.

Seventh Chakra

The seventh chakra - Sahasrara - is located at the top of the head. It is also called the "crown chakra." It represents pure, unclouded cosmic energy. Our desire to feel God is the main desire of the seventh chakra.

The unbalanced seventh chakra is a dangerous business. There is a threat that we will begin to live in an independent reality that has nothing to do with the outside world.

Surrender completely to the will of providence and submit to the Higher power. You should no longer wonder about your path. You simply live, abide in this world, and your consciousness is on a divine level.

At this level, we come to the realization that we will have to answer for our actions in the face of Eternity.

Chapter 6 The Chakra Meditation Opening Chakras in Meditation

The simplest method for identifying chakras and nadis is to simply concentrate on them, which then automatically goes to Dhyana and, at the last stage, to Samadhi. Relaxing and closing your eyes, you concentrate on one of the chosen chakras.

In all cases, the eyes should be closed at all stages of the exercise. Closing his eyes, the one who is engaged in the inner gaze directs all his attention to the area where the chakra or Nadi that interests him should be located. No other thoughts, except about this chakra (its localization, form, and properties), are unacceptable. At first, you will not see anything. Then, some heaviness, burning, or elasticity will begin to be felt in the area of the chakra. Then the chakras will begin to be felt in the form of some dense clumps. Finally, the success in the exercise will be accompanied by the "lighting" of the chakra, when the chakra chosen for today's class begins to be seen as a bright ball, glowing with the corresponding color.

In any case, the first week of classes may not even lead to the sensation of the chakras as dense clumps. You should not be upset and increase the time of your studies yourself (5-10 minutes for the first week are the limit) and even more so - you should not consider yourself unsuitable for such practice. In the first months of training in one session, you should not concentrate on more than one or a maximum of two chakras. Do not rush.

When all the chakras feel like luminous and emitting balls, it makes sense in one lesson to "look through" all of them. This is the control of the successful completion of this exercise. Such a procedure to fully identify all the major chakras along Sushumna can take 20-30 minutes. In no case should you concentrate more, since an overload of your mental and physical capabilities may occur. Over time, this restriction disappears.

The second version of the practice of exercises to identify the chakras is as follows. Having taken the initial position and relaxing, the student does not close his eyes but meditates on the graphic image of the corresponding chakra in the form of the yantra. This is the first stage of practice. It lasts no more than 5-10 minutes, similarly to the Trataka described above. All thoughts are excluded, and those that will one way or another relate to the search for bodily localization of the chakra should be preserved. At the second stage of the same exercise, the student, without rising from the mat, closes his eyes and focuses on the place where the chakra should be.

After spending as much time with his eyes closed, how much he practiced with visual fixation of the picture with the chakra, he opens his eyes again. This makes up one cycle. In one lesson, you can do from two to three such cycles. This practice option can be somewhat complicated by the fact that when closing the eyes after visual concentration in the figure of the chakra, the student tries to mentally transfer and immerse its graphic analog into the corresponding chakra.

This third option of practicing the exercise is as easy as the first two. In this case, it is advisable to open the AUM mantra with a voice or mentally at least 3 times before opening the eyes. After opening your eyes, it is useful to read some prayer formula or perform the Octagon of the Buddha. Anyway, some hard work, requiring well-known physical or intellectual efforts immediately after exercises in the identification of chakras, is categorically excluded.

I recommend reading the scriptures (for example, the Bhagavad-gita) or any other literature that is pleasant to the soul and ennobles thoughts. You should also not take a bath or go to the shower. It should be noted that the colors of the chakras that you see during successful meditation may not coincide with those colors that are given in the drawings - their graphic counterparts. The color of the revealed chakra depends both on the purity of your astral body, and on what part of the chakra you selected during the concentration process.

It should also be remembered that the exercise is called meditation, and not concentration due to the fact that in addition to highlighting the chakra itself, an attempt is made by the practitioner to determine all the related properties.

Effects of Chakra Meditation

1.   The astral body is cleansed, which leads to greater mental poise. This helps strengthen intellectual abilities, creates the conditions for unlimited growth of the mind and knowledge of the properties of the universe.

2.   The psyche becomes more flexible and controlled. At the same time, the student acquires basic prerequisites for controlling internal energy and developing the capabilities of a psychic.

3.   The ability of the sense-perception of objects of the external and especially the internal world is heightened.

4.   Eliminate the negative consequences of past mental activity. This primarily refers to meditation on the Ajna Chakra. Even in its simplest form, having not yet achieved complete success, the student receives mental rest.

Things to note

Once again, I draw your attention to the importance of observing the conditions preceding and following meditation. In addition, compliance with the principles of Yama and Niyama should be analyzed. If all these conditions are not observed, the effect may be the opposite: the psyche becomes aggravated, the consciousness becomes unbalanced and excessively nervous.

If you experience any negative feelings, proceed to reading the mantra. Until that time, when you can freely "light" the chakras, that is, during the development of the technique of exercise, you should take breaks in classes and meditate on the chakras no more than 2 times a week. The rest of the time, do lighter exercises. In any case, special attention should be paid to the Trataka, especially to the flame of a candle.

The recommended sequence for identifying chakras can be slightly modified in accordance with the principles of A. Ghosh Integral Yoga, the main of which is a ban on the activation of the lower chakras (that is, first of all, Muladhara and Swadisthana) without appropriate readiness for that from the higher chakras: Sahasrara, and Vishuddha Chakras. One way or another, the main significance here is the consolidation of the principles of Yama and Niyama in the subconscious of the practitioner, and one should always return to them with any variant of practice.

The identification of chakras and other meditative procedures of higher yogis can awaken the Kundalini. The translation of at least part of the body's static energy into a dynamic form is usually accompanied by a sensation of heat along the spine. The spine becomes hot from the inside. This sensation can be considered as a sign of the manifestation of Samadhi (the last phase of the octal ladder of the "means of achieving yoga") on the physical plane: oncoming warm and cold "waves," a cloudy veil in front of the eyes, slight dizziness, slow speech, etc. Here these processes are very probable and should not get you scared: they are objective and must pass quickly. If they do not pass, the OM mantra will help you.

In this case, the student, having adopted a meditative pose, be sure to sit cross-legged (it is very important to observe the requirement to keep your back straight!), relax and, closing his eyes, concentrate on one of the chosen chakras.

Chapter 7 Energy Healing Application

Hand Positions for Energy Healing

In the Reiki system, there are 12 main positions of the hands and 4 additional. Each of them has its own purpose in terms of healing from various diseases.

The main positions of the hands are located in the head, back, and front of the body.

The main positions for the head

The first position - Hands close the eyes

Relaxes and relieves fear and tension. It helps with problems associated with sinuses, diseases of the eyes, nose, teeth, and jaws.

Balances the pineal gland and the pituitary gland corresponding to the 6th and 7th chakra.

The second position - Hands cover the head

Synchronizes the left and right hemispheres of the brain, improves memory. Used for headaches and otitis media.

The third position - Hands cover the back of the head

It relaxes, relieves stress, and relieves mental fatigue. It is used for problems associated with the cerebellum and spinal cord, as well as headaches.

The fourth position - Hands cover the neck

It gives a feeling of joy, instills self-confidence, and enhances creative abilities. Used for tonsillitis, tonsillitis, and thyroid diseases. Corresponds to the 5th chakra.

The main positions for the front of the body

The fifth position - Hands just above the chest, at heart level

It creates a feeling of love, trust, and spiritual harmony. It affects the thymus corresponding to the heart chakra.

Useful for the lungs and cardiovascular system.

The sixth position - Hands at the level of the solar plexus

Relieves from fears and worries caused by stress. Affects the solar plexus corresponding to the 3rd chakra. It is used for diseases of the liver, stomach, gall bladder, spleen, and digestive tract.

The seventh position - Hands on the stomach

It helps to get rid of stress and unfounded fears. It affects the 2nd and 3rd chakras. It is used for diseases of the liver, stomach, gall bladder, spleen, and digestive tract.

The eighth position - Lower abdomen

Relieves of sexual impotence and relieves stress associated with insecurity in sexual capabilities.

It has an effect on the 1st and 2nd chakras. It is useful for women for the ovaries and uterus, for men - for the prostate gland.

It helps with diseases of the digestive tract.

The main positions for the back

The ninth position - Hands at the base of the neck

It relieves stress and promotes relaxation. It helps with problems in the spine and neck.

The tenth position - Arms at shoulder level

It has the same effect as the ninth position for the front surface of the body.

The eleventh position - Hands on the back

It has the same effect as the seventh position. It affects the 2nd and 3rd chakras.

Useful for the kidneys.

The twelfth position - Hands at the base of the spine

It has the same effect as the eighth position. It has an effect on the 1st and 2nd chakras.

Useful for tailbone injuries.

Additional positions First position

One hand is on the forehead, the other on the back of the head. This position is also called the "cosmic plug" because it helps to "recharge" your energy or the energy of the person you are healing.

Second position

One hand is on the heart chakra; the other is on the face. This position helps with insomnia: it allows you to calm down and fall asleep.

Third position

Both hands are on the heart chakra. This position also contributes to rapid falling asleep.

Fourth position

One hand is on the heart chakra; the other is on the solar plexus. It acts the same as in the first position.

Experiencing Presence - Treatment Session Conditions

Ventilate the room well before starting a treatment session. It should be clean, bright, and quiet so that you can relax well. If the room you choose does not particularly meet these requirements, before starting treatment, clean the energy in it using the Reiki method.

Prepare a blanket in advance in case you feel cold during relaxation. You can also use soothing music.

Wash your hands in advance if you have to touch the person you are healing. In addition, you need to cleanse yourself of the low vibrations of energy in your hands.

Rub your hands to warm them.

Both you and your patient must remove the watch if you do not want the time displayed on it to change under the influence of Reiki energy.

You, as a person transmitting energy, remove everything from your hands so as not to injure the patient during touch.

The healed must take off what constricts his body — a belt, tie, and bra. As for jewelry: it is better to remove chains and bracelets. Removing rings and earrings are not necessary, as they are charged with good energy.

The patient should lie or sit comfortably. You must definitely relax. Do not cross arms or legs and try to free yourself from tension.

If you cannot touch the healed, keep your hands above the person. Keep your hands 3-5 cm above body areas that should not be touched due to burns or skin diseases. You can put your hands on top of clothes or a wool blanket. If it's uncomfortable to touch some areas, put your hands on this area over the hands of the recipient.

Tell the patient in advance about the changes that may occur after treatment. He should know that immediately after a healing session, his condition may worsen, unpleasant symptoms such as fever, nervous excitement, more profuse discharge, eczema or pain may appear. These phenomena are called an improvement reaction, indicating that the process of restoring health has begun.

Reiki exercises

Those who are just starting to practice Reiki can be advised on simple exercises that are directly related to the teachings of Mikao Usui. They will be very helpful in the preparatory phase. Basically, they are associated with relaxation, by learning which, you can at any moment, barely feeling tired, fully relax.

The state of rest does not occur on its own. It may seem strange to you, but you need to learn this. Without the ability to relax, Reiki may seem to you too complicated a practice - not getting rid of fatigue, but, on the contrary, an excessive waste of strength and energy.

You can contact the complex below at any time as soon as you feel tired. You can also use it as protective gymnastics to recover from a Reiki session you do for someone else.

Exercise 1

Sit on a comfortable (medium-hard) mat. Cross your legs. Keep your back and head straight. Cover your eyelids and look in front of you. The abdominal muscles are tense, and the upper body is relaxed. Keep your hands on your stomach - one slightly higher than the other. The breathing is even calm.

Your task is to direct energy to the area just below the navel and mentally focus on this point.

Exercise 2

Cross your fingers and hold them by the head, hold on the back of the head. Press lightly on the back of the head. As you exhale, relax. Perform the exercise for 5-10 minutes. It not only helps to relax but also relieves dizziness.

Exercise 3

Release your fingers and pinch your auricles. Press with your index fingers on the points located just above the auricles. Place your thumbs in position behind the ear. Do this exercise 5 times.

Exercise 4

Slowly lower your arms down. Then place them near the abdomen so that the palm of one hand touches the back of the other. Cross your legs. Tilt your head forward a bit. Swing your head from side to side. Do this about 10 times.

Shaking your head has a powerful healing effect. It leads to the massage of points located behind the ear. This exercise is an excellent prevention of various diseases of the eyes, ear, throat, nose, as well as neurasthenia.

Exercise 5

Performing the previous exercise, you can feel an unpleasant heaviness in the back. The reason is the stagnant processes. In order to get rid of negative feelings, you need to give the spinal and lumbar muscles the necessary tone. This is done by rubbing the points located on the lower back.

A massage is performed in a sitting position. Cross your legs and keep your back straight. Take a few deep breaths. Mentally direct energy to the navel. Then hold your breath. At this point, you will feel the heat spreading inside the abdomen. Spread your hands, as before self-massage, and with warm fingers touch the lower back. Lightly stroke the points near the lower parts of the spine. Do this 10 times.

Exercise 6

Stay in a sitting position. Keep your back and head straight. Pull the legs forward so that the heels touch and the toes point up. Bend your arms at the elbows - so that the palms are pointing down. Do not strain.

Describe the circle in the air as if you were spinning a wheel. Hand movements begin in the lower abdomen and then to the hypochondrium. Fingers should be free.

This exercise relieves fatigue in the legs and at the same time, has a therapeutic effect on diseases of the lower back.

Exercise 7

Sit with your legs extended and touching the heels on the floor. Squeeze your fingers into a lock and raise your hands above your head with your palms up. Stay in this position for a few seconds, and then touch the crown of your head with your fingers. Keep your head straight, slightly extend the spine up. Relax your hands and touch your toes. Try not to bend your knees, but do not strain. Repeat exercise 5 times.

It is aimed at relaxation and rest, and in addition, when it is performed, the muscles of the chest, legs, and arms are filled with energy.

Exercise 8

Take a sitting position. Keep your back and head straight. Look in front of you with your eyes half-closed. Keep your hands in the lower abdomen, one palm over the other. Take a few full breaths. Calm down and tune into contemplation. Concentrate on the point in the navel. Abdominal breathing. Thanks to this exercise, you will feel an influx of heat into the abdomen, which means restoring the balance of yin and yang.

And here are a few more exercises aimed at restoring the balance of elements and relieving stress. They are performed in the famous yoga position "Lotus."

Exercise 9

Sit on the floor. Stretch your legs. Keep your torso straight. Imagine your spine is the axis from earth to sky. Keep your hands on your lap. Bend the left leg at the knee, turn its foot with the sole upward, and place it on the thigh of the right leg at the groin. You need to touch the back of the foot. Bend the right leg at the knee, and put the foot on the thigh of the left leg in the groin area (backside). Both knees should be pressed to the floor.

If it doesn't work right away, don't worry. Achieve perfection gradually. When you take the desired position with ease, know that you are at the goal. In this case, the effect of breathing exercises will increase significantly; rhythmic breathing will appear. You will stock up on creative energy; you will feel its surge in your body. If your breath is directed towards enlightenment, then you can hold back the energy that overflows you. Then it will serve only for your good - it will create a barrier to illnesses, bad thoughts, and deeds.

Exercise 10

Lie on your back. Stretch your legs, and place your hands along the body. In succession, relax all the muscles, starting from the legs - feet, lower legs, knees, hips, and then - the trunk, arms, shoulders, neck, head.

Breathe smoothly, calmly, without straining. At some point, you will stop feeling your body. Consciousness will concentrate on the inner workings of the heart. You will feel that you are immersed in a state of absolute peace and joy. Try to breathe as slowly as you can, but do not do it too consciously. The right pace will come on its own.

Exercise 11

Take a sitting or standing position. The eyes are half-closed. The breath is even measured. Focus on the point just below the navel. Hands up. As you inhale, feel the life-giving energy approach you. As you exhale, lower your arms - so that the palms are turned toward the body. In this case, mentally imagine the channels of energy passage and remove all blocks from its path. The spent energy will go to the ground through the legs.

As you inhale, let the energy rise again. Hands up. Repeat the exercise several times. It opens the chakras, which is necessary for the effectiveness of Reiki.

Learn How to be Mindful During Energy Healing
All of the above exercises allow you to fully absorb Reiki and make the most of the opportunity open to you to improve your condition - both yours and other people.

The practice of Reiki involves a special attitude towards the purification of the soul. This allows you to distance yourself from all situations and emotions that distract the mind. You may well resort to such mindfulness practices at the end of the day when you feel tired.

Chapter 8 Practical Classes For You!

Mr. Mikao Usui's Reiki's natural healing method is based on three pillars - Gassho, Reiji Ho, and Tiryo.

Gassho

At the end of each meditation or healing technique, Gassho's position is used, which in Japanese means "two hands joined together." Keep your palms at chest level, or rather, at heart level, which will be an expression of gratitude to God or the Universe.

Take a lotus or half lotus pose.

Close your eyes and relax. If you can, keep your eyes closed all the time to save energy inside and not be distracted by external stimuli.

Try to keep your back as straight as possible, but do not strain. If it's hard or uncomfortable for you to sit like that, you can put something under your back.

Do not regulate breathing; just let air in and out. Inhale deeply into the stomach.

Concentrate all your attention on the tips of your middle fingers (or on the tanden) and forget about everything else.

Do not drive away thoughts. Look at them from the side, be aware of them, and then again focus on your fingertips.

If you feel that your hands are tired, then slowly, without opening your palms, put them on your knees, and then return them to their original position.

At the end of the session, open your eyes and shake well your hands.

Thanks to gassho meditation, an increase in energy and an addiction to a meditative state of mind occur. Gassho should be performed every day - in the morning and/or in the evening - for 20-30 minutes.

Reiji ho

Translated from Japanese, the word "reiji" means "definition of the spirit," and in our case - "definition of Reiki energy." This technique teaches us to follow our intuition. It is to follow, not develop because intuition as a divine gift is given to us at birth. Our business is only to learn to hear her voice and act as he tells us.

As for the Reiji technique, just let the energy live freely. Feel like an empty vessel, which itself, without any participation from you, will be filled with vital energy. Do not think about where, when, and how it enters you; everything will happen by itself.

Sit or stand in front of the person you want to heal from some kind of ailment. Close your eyes and fold your hands in Gassho.

Focus your attention on tanden. Get rid of any stress and relax. Feel how your body is filled with Reiki energy and how you become part of this energy.

Ask your patient to be aware of the causes of his ailments, failures. Then ask for his healing at all levels. Slowly move your hands to the "third eye" area and ask Reiki to bring your hands where you need to. Problem areas will call your hands for help themselves.

Now you just have to wait a bit. You will certainly feel where your hands should go. This can happen in different ways. If visual images are closer to you, then you will see that part of the body that needs to be treated. If you tend to perceive the world by ear, you will hear this information. If you are a kinesthetic, that is, you perceive the world as if it were pores of the skin, then you just feel where you should touch the patient.

You can receive a "message" immediately or after some time. In order to speed up this process, place one or both of your hands on the patient's crown chakra and tune in to the energy of his body. If you still can't feel the problem area, use the Beesen technique (we will talk about it a bit later).

However, you must be assured that regular training will do the trick: you will learn to identify problem areas much faster, and when practicing Reiki for several years, you will see them with a bare glance at the person.

"How do you recognize this answer?" you ask. It comes to everyone differently. You yourself will feel it by a slight tingling sensation in your hands, a feeling of warmth or magnetism, or maybe you simply realize that the answer is received.

The art of Reiji Ho is akin to creativity: starting to use it for healing, you can extend your skill to any other areas of your life.

Tiryo

Translated into English, the word "tiryo" means "treatment." The patient lies on the floor or on any bedding. The healer kneels next to him and holds his dominant hand over his parietal chakra until there is an impulse or inspiration, which is followed by a hand.

The healer gives his hands complete freedom. It refers to the painful areas of the patient's body until they cease to hurt or until the hands themselves are detached from the body and find a new area for treatment.

Reiki Meditations

To elevate the spirit and heal the body in Reiki, special techniques are used that use the energy of higher dimensions and the accumulation of light.

Meditation (in the lane with Latin. - Reflection) is an internal concentration and concentration of the mind, control of one's own   thought processes. Historically, meditative techniques have appeared in various religious practices (Buddhism, Sufism, Judaism, and Taoism). Nowadays, they are widely used in psychotherapy as a method of mental relaxation.

Along with the direct healing effect, meditation affects the deepest spiritual layers of human life. It opens up access to those innermost depths of the personality that are buried in everyday life under everyday worries and problems or are carefully covered with all kinds of social masks. With the help of meditation, we seem to establish a dialogue between consciousness and the subconscious; we allow the content of the subconscious to "surface" and manifest itself in consciousness. Meditative practice contributes to the development of intuition, which will undoubtedly be useful to any of us in everyday life and in creativity.

The method of meditation can also be used to combat stress.

Meditative techniques give both quick psychotherapeutic results and long- term ones. Experience shows that even short classes in meditative practices have a positive effect on human health. With long classes, of course, a greater effect is obtained. People who use the method of meditation both independently and under the supervision of a specialist have a more stable nervous system. They are less anxious and better manage stress.

In order to master the method of meditation, you need to practice regularly; then, it will become a familiar tool in self-medication.

In this case, it is necessary to control breathing, muscle tone, emotions, the flow of thoughts, and attention - the psychophysical components of meditation.

Muscle Tone Control

You can determine the depth of stress by muscle tension: the stronger the stress, the higher the muscle tension. With depression, the tone of the respiratory muscles' decreases, and with anxiety and fear, the tone of the occipital muscles and muscle groups associated with speech increases. In other words, in order to relieve stress and normalize the psychophysical state, it is necessary to achieve relaxation of the muscles that affect the state of rest and rest.

Deep muscle relaxation leads to the release of substances with anti-stress action and stimulating the centers of pleasure of the brain - endorphins. Activation of the pleasure mechanism not only gives a pleasant feeling of relaxation but can also be considered as a preventive measure against stress.

Breath Control

First, learn how to regulate inhalation and exhalation. This will help you when you start practicing Reiki. To do this, take a regular, natural breath. Mentally pass your life energy to the navel area, as if deepening into the intestines. Hold your breath for a couple of seconds. Exhale - continuously, slowly, making the sound "Ha." The mouth is slightly ajar. Relax. Repeat this cycle 10-15 times.

A person in a stressful situation is characterized by superficial (shallow), fast or intermittent chest breathing, and slow abdominal breathing in a state of rest and comfort. Typically, the breathing process is automatic, and through meditation, you can learn to carefully monitor your breathing and be aware of it. Thanks to meditation, we can maintain abdominal breathing and mentally direct it to the desired area of the body, thus neutralizing anxiety, agitation, and outbreaks of negative emotions. In other words, we ourselves are able to give ourselves the opportunity to calm down in a situation of sudden short-term stress.

In meditation, breathing through some part of the body is often used. What does this mean? How can you breathe through some part of the body? It goes without saying that this is not about physiological breathing, but about the imaginary, existing only in our view. And if, as a result of meditation, you have a feeling of "extrapulmonary" breathing. A temporary connection has been established between two parts of the brain - the one that receives information from the respiratory tract and the respiratory muscles, and the one that receives information from the corresponding area of the body that is not connected with breathing.

As a result of changes in sensations in a selected part of the body, in particular, rhythmic fluctuations in their intensity occur synchronously with the phases of the respiratory cycle (attenuation of intensity - by inspiration, amplification - by exhalation). Such a temporary connection between different foci of excitation in the brain helps us fight pain, control our own pulse or blood pressure, and improve our mood.

How to understand whether you are doing the meditation exercise correctly? The criterion is the synchronization of breathing and sensations in a selected part of the body.

As we have said, this is an increase in inspiration and a decrease in exhalation. With excitement or sudden fear, the ratio of inspiratory time to the time of the respiratory cycle increases as the inspiration becomes longer. Accordingly, a person in a state of relaxation is characterized by an inverse relationship. In meditation, the function of a longer expiration is used to more fully relax and calm emotions - muscle relaxation exactly at the time of exhalation.

In many meditations, the method of breathing through the hands is used. The fact is that palms and fingers play a very special role in our bodies. The area occupied by the projection area of the hand is larger than any other part of the body. Therefore, focusing on the sensations associated with the hands captures a much larger area of the cerebral cortex than for any other part of the body, and accordingly has a greater effect on the state of the brain and consciousness.

Emotion Control

With the help of breathing, we can not only monitor our emotions but also manage them. Our task is to learn to control our emotions. This is not so difficult: you need to feel your own body and grasp any changes associated with emotions. Our mistake lies in the fact that we often perceive only the information that comes from the outside, and completely ignore the signals coming from the inside. We do not seem to notice that we live in our own bodies.

Self-observation is, in essence, the ability to stay in the "here and now" state, on which the Reiki method is based.

Thought Flow Control

With the help of directed attention, calm breathing, and muscle relaxation, you can control the flow of thoughts. Decreased muscle tone reduces the flow of information from the muscles to the brain, allowing it to rest. Partial liberation of brain neurons from information processing leads to a special, or, as they say, altered, state of consciousness, which, in fact, plays a healing role.

How does this happen? In a state of altered state of consciousness achieved through deep meditation, the asymmetry between the hemispheres disappears. There comes a kind of condition without time and space, where the most controversial internal problems of the body are resolved - both psychological and physiological.

To enter an altered state of consciousness, you must do the following:

- Focus on inner feelings. This will reduce the influx of external stimuli to the brain, thereby helping to escape from the outside world and plunge into the depths of the inner world.

-      Breathe in a measured rhythm, forcing attention to follow yourself and helping to direct it to certain parts of the body.

-      Achieve muscle relaxation to reduce the flow of information from the muscles to the brain and help it sink into a state of rest.

As a result of immersion in this altered state, the roles are redistributed between consciousness and the subconscious. In the ordinary, awake state, our subconscious mind is suppressed by consciousness. In an altered state, consciousness, as it were, goes by the wayside, and the subconscious, on the contrary, is sharply activated.

Unexpectedly mobilizing reserves of the subconscious helps us solve important external problems. Due to the formation of new ties that expand the narrow framework of stereotypic response, the resolution of internal psychological problems also occurs.

An altered state of consciousness gives us the opportunity to relax, relieve the effects of stress. The body's natural regenerative processes are activated to help cure stress-related diseases.

Meditation is sometimes called the gap between thoughts. It seems that the internal dialogue ceases, there is a "stuck" on unresolved problems, a state of inner peace sets in, allowing you to know yourself, listen to the voice of the subconscious. This path to the inner wisdom that helps us find a way out of a difficult situation at first seems very difficult. But as you master the meditative practice, it becomes easier and comes to automatism.

Breathing Techniques

Many underestimate the role of breathing in Reiki practice. It is not right. After all, breathing is not just a process of inhaling, exhaling. It is directly related to vitality. In order for the energy to work for the good, you need to master several methods of proper breathing. You can choose one of them that will not cause difficulties.

What is "proper breathing"? It is distinguished by naturalness, measuredness, concentration, and evenness. In this case, you can breathe in different ways: inhaling and exhaling through the nose, or inhaling through the nose, and exhaling through the mouth, or inhaling and exhaling through the nose and mouth. Consciousness, at the same time, should concentrate on deep and rhythmic breathing. The mind prevails in this case. Every movement and every breath is controlled by it.

Remember that breathing exercises should not cause tension or dizziness. If this still happened, stop doing the exercise and breathe normally. Never allow violence against yourself! Remember that your breath is one of the sides of the whole being created.

Cleansing Breath

Stand up straight. Legs together. The palms are pressed to each other. The wrists are slightly pressed on the stomach so that the palms are perpendicular to the body. Take a deep breath through your nose. Hold your breath for a moment and start exhaling. In this case, the lips fold into a tube. Then, rhythmically, with strong, but sharp exhalations, throw out the air. Make sharp sounds. Do not puff out your cheeks.

This method of breathing cleanses the lungs and refreshes the body, gives it a reserve of vigor and health.

"Ha" - Breath

"Ha" breathing cleanses the respiratory system and helps improve blood flow. It also helps to keep calm and eliminate feelings of depression.

Stand straight - legs together, toes slightly apart. Take a deep breath. As you inhale, slowly raise your arms above your head, palms forward. Hands should be relaxed. Hold your breath. Then lower your hands and swiftly lean forward - so that your hands almost touch the floor. Exhale sharply through the mouth, saying "Ha" without the help of the vocal cords. Sound is produced by exhaled air. Thus, you are freed from negative energy - it goes down through the hands. Stay in the tilt position for a few seconds - until the next breath. As you inhale, slowly straighten up, raising your arms above your head. With an exhalation through the nose, take the starting position. Repeat the exercise again.

Breath for Clarifying Thinking

This breathing exercise improves brain activity, increases the clarity of consciousness, and activates the thought process. The main role here is given to the diaphragm. Everything is built not on inhalation, but on exhalation.

Accept the Lotus position. If this is difficult for you to do, take any sitting posture. First, exhale sharply and quickly through your nose. After that - a full breath, just as fast and strong. No breath holding is required. Exhalation is done through the movement of the abdominal muscles and diaphragm (similar to the work of blacksmith bellows). Air fills the middle and lower parts of the lungs.

After exhaling, relax your abdominal muscles. The diaphragm will also be relaxed, and the lungs will be able to go down. First, do the exercise 10 times, and gradually bring it to 100.

Calming Breath

Soothing breath - smooth and deep. It can also be called natural. It usually complements the complete relaxation of the body. During such breathing, all your anxieties go away. You begin to feel that living is easy and enjoyable. You learn to mentally direct energy as you need.

Stretched breathing is also natural, but you should try to extend the breathing cycle a bit. On inhalation, touch the palate with your tongue. Lead energy to the lower body (just below the navel). Then hold your breath for a couple of seconds. Take a long exhalation, freeing the lungs. Do all this and mentally. Mouth ajar. Hold your breath again for a couple of seconds and exhale.

Deep Breathing

Deep breathing stimulates all endocrine glands, especially the thyroid gland. Metabolism improves. Such qualities as the ability to concentrate, the speed of reaction, and thinking develop.

Attention! This exercise cannot be performed at high pressure.

Accept the Lotus position. If it not yet comfortable for you to take this position, you can stand, sit, or lie.

Concentrate on the thyroid gland. Take a full breath through your nose for every 8th pulse beat. Hold your breath for the same length of time. Then exhale completely through your mouth, making a whistling sound. Do not tighten your lips. The duration of exhalation is twice as long, so the proportion "inhale-hold of breath-exhale" is 1: 1: 2. Repeat exercise 5 times.

Abdominal Breathing

Abdominal breathing leads to the active work of the diaphragm, which means that it becomes easier to work with the lungs. It is also beneficial for blood flow to the spleen and pancreas. Cells are actively enriched with oxygen, which has a positive effect on the brain.

The first way - Take a breath - as you feel comfortable. The tongue should be located in the mouth so that the middle part slightly touches the palate, and with the tip - touch the teeth. Mentally direct life force below the navel. Focus on this area and hold your breath. On inspiration, try to maximize the size of the lower abdomen. Open your mouth slightly and exhale. The lower abdomen is compressed, and your attention is focused on the area below the navel.

The second way - Take a breath, as in method one. Also, direct life force to the lower abdomen. The abdomen does not protrude, but contracts. Focus on the bottom of it.

Hold your breath for a few seconds, and then exhale according to the same rules as in the first case. Hold your breath again. Focus on the navel.

These exercises can be complicated with the help of meditative phrases such as: "I feel good and calm,"; "I am in peace and harmony,"; "I am balanced," and others. Mentally pronounce the first part of the phrase when the tongue touches the palate. The lower abdomen increases in size. As you exhale, touch the tip of your tongue to your teeth and speak the second part of the phrase. The stomach is compressed and remains a couple of seconds in this position.

There is a variant of exercise when inhalation is done through the nose and exhale through the mouth. Repeat the exercise slowly and measuredly.

Primal Breath (Fetal Breathing)
A person's breathing is usually a reflection of his lifestyle. People who are in a hurry all the time breathe shallowly. Those who have the opportunity to contemplate breathe deeply. But each of us had a period of maximum comfort and protection from the stresses of the outside world - a period of stay in the mother's womb. Therefore, exercises that restore initial breathing are very effective.

Focus on the area below the navel.

Send life energy there. Its penetration is controlled by a thought that is focused on it. As you inhale, squeeze your stomach, hold your breath and exhale slowly. As you exhale, relax your muscles. Hold your breath out and take a breath again. Such breath is given to us by Nature.

You can combine complete breathing, covering all body parts, with the conduit of energy. This will allow your body to get the maximum energy necessary for healing energy and for life.

Take a full, deep breath. Move vitality from the navel along the legs to the main point, which is located between the pads of the foot. Hold your breath and then exhale - slowly and completely. The energy at the same time rises up - from the feet to the lower abdomen.

This method of breathing will lead to the maximum enrichment of your body with oxygen and the removal of processed products. The work of the heart is normalized. The functioning of the respiratory and circulatory systems will improve. This breath can be called the "breath of youth."

There is also a method that includes the whole body in a breath- exhale cycle. Focus on the area below the navel. On inhalation, vital energy spreads throughout the body. Hold your breath for a couple of seconds. On exhalation, vital energy is carried out from the area below the navel throughout the body. As you exhale, hold your breath. With this method of breathing, all cells of the body are filled with life-giving force, which leads to their rejuvenation.

Full Breath

Full breathing activates the entire respiratory apparatus. With this method of breathing, energy consumption is significantly saved. All muscles work, the diaphragm is completely free, is not clamped by anything, and, therefore, actively helps air exchange processes.

Full breathing allows you to accumulate a large amount of energy in the body, increases the useful volume of the lungs. It calms the nervous system and promotes the development of will and determination. The functioning of the endocrine system improves, and hence the metabolism, which leads to the rejuvenation of the body.

Accept any position - lying, sitting, or standing. Exhale, trying to do so as fully as possible. Inhale through the nose.

Inhalation should be done for every 8th pulse beat, so that in a cycle of inhalation - breath-holding - exhalation, a proportion of 2: 1: 2 is observed. In this position, hold your breath for 4 heartbeats. Then start exhaling -

slowly, following the same sequence as when inhaling. First, air goes through the nose, the abdominal walls are drawn in, then the ribs are compressed, and the shoulders and collarbones are lowered.

Directed Attention

Thanks to the ability to direct attention to various parts of the body, the appearance of a stable "image of oneself," or, speaking the language of physiologists, "body patterns" is achieved. This awareness affects both the person's self-esteem and his relationship with others.

Focused exercise has more than a healing effect. They provide an opportunity to quickly recover after sudden stress, at a time when emotional balance and self-control are lost. These exercises free us from panic and all kinds of fears.

The essence of the exercises is to mentally move to certain boundaries, which we will now mention. We can say that we are, as it were, attached to reality by both ends of the body: below - through contact with the ground, above - through the crown of the head.

In Taoist meditation practices, special attention is paid to the following boundaries: the crown - to enhance the sensation of ascending flows of "energy" (the border "man-sky"); palms - to reproduce the feeling of emphasis in the fingers and palms (the "man-man" border) and feet — to enhance the feeling of downward flows of "energy" (the "man-earth" border).

Exercises come down to taking a few deep breaths and exhaling and switching attention alternately to each of the indicated boundaries, starting with the "earth."

You probably already understood that all the psychophysiological components of meditation are closely related. Calm, slow breathing, muscle relaxation, and directed attention lead to calming thoughts and normalize the psychophysical consciousness of a person.

Meditative practices can be applied in everyday life. If you conduct them constantly, you will develop self-regulation skills that will give you peace and well-being. You will learn to control emotions and thoughts, and therefore, will adequately respond to any events.

From the foregoing, it follows that meditation is an integral part of the Reiki energy healing method.

Chapter 9 Unique Reiki Healing Practices

Before meditation or healing begins, it is necessary to activate three energy centers, or, as they are called in the Taoist tradition, three Dan-tien. This is necessary in order to further focus on its

connection with the energy of the Earth and the energy of the Universe. Indeed, at the initial stage, you are not accustomed to energy flows, and you need to learn how to train the state of deep immersion of attention "inside yourself." Then this will happen automatically: in a split second, you will feel your connection with the Earth and the Universe.

In general, the concept of the three main energy centers (reservoirs) of a person is one of the basic concepts in Reiki. The philosopher from the sacred mountain of Kurama, Dr. Usui, teaches that in the Universe there are three main forces - Light, Love, and Power, for the harmonious functioning of which it is necessary to observe their balance. Light, Love, and Strength are represented in man by three Tributes (Tribute is concentrated energy). If you live in harmony with Love, Light, and Power, you will find happiness. The upper Dan-tien is in the head. Using the power of the Spirit, it provides the interaction of the microcosm with the flows of Universal and Cosmic energy.

Middle Dan-tien is located in the middle of the body, at the level of the heart center. It provides an internal interaction of forces, is a container of love and virtue.

Lower Dan-tien, which is also called the "internal battery," is located between the navel, kidney and sexual centers. In Japanese tradition, this place is called tanden. With its help, the interaction of the microcosm with the flow of Earth energy is provided. In the lower Dan-tian, energy from all sources is mixed and converted into life force. This area contains many large lymph nodes, such as the lumbar lymph, common ileal, main drainage canal in the lower abdomen. An increase in the amount of energy in this area enhances blood flow, the movement of lymph and hormones, and saves the heart from unnecessary work.

Here is the area of the kidneys, which is also very important. The normal functioning of the kidneys in eastern folk medicine is given great attention since their condition affects the functioning of other body systems.

Thus, the physical health of a person, his sexual abilities, life expectancy depend on the quantity and quality of energy in tanden.

Concentrating on tanden is used in all Reiki techniques. By focusing on the tanden area, we can gradually restore our core energy.

Kenyoku

Translated from Japanese, "kenyoku" means "dry shower." The purpose of Kenyoku meditation is to cleanse the soul and body of negative thoughts and emotions in which we are immersed so much that we have no opportunity for self-disclosure.

We worry about all kinds of problems - both our own and others' - and miss the moments in life that will never happen again. But Kenyoku just allows us to feel the real, only moment.

This original technique should be performed every time you return home to free yourself from everyday fuss. Kenyoku meditation is carried out before each healing session, energy exercise, and at the end of the healing session.

It is performed in a sitting, standing, or lying position. The hand either touches the body or is located at a distance of 10 cm from the body.

In Reiki practice, three variations of this technique are used.

Option One

1.   Place the open palm of your right hand on your left shoulder. The fingertips are opposite the top of the shoulder, where the collarbone meets the shoulder. Run your open palm in a straight line through the sternum to the upper right thigh. Repeat this action on the right side using your left hand, and then do the same thing on the left side again.

2.   Place your right hand on top of your left shoulder. Slide your open palm on the outside with your straight left hand to your fingertips. Repeat this with your right hand, and then, if you want, again with your left.

Option Two

1.   See paragraph 1 of the first option.

2.   Sweep the open palm of one hand with the open palm of the other hand.

Option Three

1.   See paragraph 1 of the first option.

2.   Swipe movements with the open palm of one hand on the inside of the other hand, from the shoulder to the tips of the fingers.

Any of these options for Kenyoku ends with Gassho's position.

Joshin Kokyu Ho

Translated from Japanese, "Joshin Kokyu Ho" means "breath that cleanses the soul." The main goal of this meditation is complete relaxation, which will help you absorb cosmic energies with all organs and harmonize them. Only in this way can the best results in recovery be achieved. Joshin Kokyu Ho meditation is primarily aimed at relaxing the "third eye" area (the eyebrows).

This original technique is performed standing, sitting, or lying down.

Breathe slowly and naturally. Allow your body to relax and allow Reiki energy to flow completely freely.

Activate energy centers.

Put your hands on your hips with your palms up and breathe naturally through your nose. Focus on the lower energy center (tanden). As you inhale, imagine the white light entering the crown chakra, which will descend into the tanden, accumulate there and begin to gradually spread throughout the body, dissolving all tension. As you exhale, imagine how the white light that fills your entire body radiates through the skin, saturating and strengthening your aura.

A light flow of thought, minimal involvement of consciousness, and focus on sensations will appear, and

Reiki energy will enter the body through the crown and exit through the pores.

This exercise takes a few minutes, but you can do it as much as you want. Finish it in the Gassho position and shake afterward, your hands.

Zakikiri Zoka Ho

This original technique of "cleansing objects" (this is how Zakikiri Dzoka Ho is translated from Japanese) allows you to remove strong negative energy and restore vibrational order using Reiki energy. Usually, this technique is used to charge crystals, amulets, and other items.

Your task is to activate the three energy centers.

Put the selected item on the palm of your left hand (and if you're left- handed, then right). If the subject is too large and does not fit in your palm, then the technique should be applied at certain points.

Say out loud: "I am starting Dzakikiri Dzoka Ho."

Constantly focus your attention on the lower Dan-tien.

Swipe your right palm at a distance of 5 cm from the subject, and then abruptly stop movement and hold your breath.

Do this manipulation 3 times, and then let Reiki fill this item through your hands.

When finished, set aside the item you were working with. Fold your hands in the position of Gassho and say: "I have finished Zakikiri Zoka Ho." Shake your hands well.

If you want, you can repeat this meditation again. In general, carry out such cleaning of objects as necessary.

Reiki Undo

The Japanese word "undo" means "exercise." In this case, we mean an exercise that frees the body from blocks and tension, allowing it to move without restrictions. This technique is performed while standing or sitting.

You will have to make circular motions for about 35 minutes, and therefore, for a start, you need to find a suitable place where no one will bother you and where there are no sharp corners that can cause injury.

Fold your hands in Gassho and mentally say: "Reiki Undo begins." So you allow Reiki energy to flow freely into your body.

Activate the three energy centers (Tribute).

Take a deep breath and exhale completely relax.

Now take another deep breath and as you exhale try to let out as much air as possible.

By conducting such inhalations and exhalations several times, you may feel that your body has begun to move. If movement is difficult, be patient and continue to do this exercise daily for 3 months. If you find it difficult to completely relax, try to imagine that you are not an adult, but a child who can act the way he wants. Forget about self-control and remember that no one is looking at you. Throw all thoughts out of your head and indulge in a children's game.

If any sounds fly off your lips, do not shut up. If any memories come or emotions flow, do not drive them back, but rather, be aware of them and feel them. If tears flow from your eyes, do not hold back - cry as much as you want. Your kind of open up and let off steam: letting your body clear. Do not worry, it itself knows what and how to do it. The main thing is not to limit your healing, to eliminate all prohibitions. Continue until your movements stop themselves.

When this happens, sit down or lie down. Immerse yourself deeply in yourself and observe the movement of energy within you. You may feel like you have stopped feeling the boundaries of your physical body. Fold your hands in Gassho and mentally say: "I graduated from Reiki Undo." Thank the energy of Reiki, and shake it well with your hands.

Reiki Shower

This technique is very simple and effective. You can apply it when you need to quickly cleanse yourself, restore energy balance, and fill up with Reiki energy.

Stand up or sit back. Close your eyes. Breathe easy and relaxed. When inhaling, raise your hands up, and as you exhale, slowly lower them with your palms towards you.

Activate the three energy centers (Tribute).

When you inhale, you absorb the energy of Reiki, and as you exhale, it passes through the whole body, purifying and healing it. At the same time, unused energy, together with our negative energy, goes to the earth.

We can say it another way: when you inhale, you raise the energy of the Earth and pass it through the body, and when you exhale, you give it to Heaven. By completing the exercise, you transfer the energy of Heaven to Earth.

Repeat the exercise several times, joining hands in Gassho.

Reiki Mawashi

The word "mawashi" in translation from Japanese means "current." Reiki mawashi is a group exercise with the current Reiki energy that passes through the bodies of the participants in the exercise.

Sit in a circle and hold your hands a few centimeters above or near the hand of each of your neighbors left and right.

If it's more convenient for you to touch your hands, then, please.

Turn your left palm up and the right palm down. The teacher sets the flow of energy to the left. Left hand, palm up. The receiver takes energy with his right hand, palm turned down, conducts energy through his body, and gives it to the next participant through his left hand. Interestingly, the energy of the group often exceeds the sum of the energies of all participants. It spontaneously heals at all possible levels.

The technique is performed within 10-15 minutes.

Healing Practices

In addition to the meditative practices of Reiki, there are also healing practices.

When self-meditating, you need to put your hands on your body in the indicated order (or hold them above the body). You will go through all the main positions or those that you consider necessary. To touch places that are hard to reach, such as those located on your back, simply put your hands nearby and imagine that they are in the correct position. Then the energy of Reiki will go exactly to the place you are thinking about. After all, it is able to pass either through the hands or through the realization that healing is directed to a certain position.

The time for transferring Reiki energy to the main positions for those who have passed the first stage is basically 5 minutes. Thus, in an hour, you can go through all 12 positions. However, do not get hung up on just this time: determine how much you personally need it.

After you have sent Reiki to all the main positions, put your hands on the sore spots. If you do not have enough time, put your hands on the sore spot immediately after directing energy to the head area. Remove your hands when you feel some effect - healing or at least relief. You can carry out such treatment at any time and in any place. If you have no time, you need not fulfill all 12 positions of Reiki treatment, but do them separately at different times. However, if you want to achieve complete harmony, you will have to complete all 12 positions.

It's all about self-healing. But you can treat other people with Reiki's help. To do this, put your hands on each of the positions on the other person's body and keep them there for 5 minutes, that is, the same way as in self-treatment.

If you want to direct energy to any one position or to a place that causes concern to your patient, first direct Reiki energy to the head area, and then to this position.

With the help of Reiki energy, you can also heal animals. First, put your hand on your pet's forehead, and then move on to other positions on his head and body. If you cannot touch any place or hold your hands firmly, hold them just a short distance away. The animal will feel calm and comfortable when during the transfer of energy, you gently put your hands on his head or neck.

If you want to cure a bird, carefully grab it with both your hands or keep your hands above the cage. You can even treat your aquarium fish with your hands on the aquarium!

To treat a plant, place your hands on its leaves, trunk, or roots. Flowers heal as follows: the stems or roots are held with both hands. You can send Reiki vital energy to the seeds of plants or vegetables, or you can send it to the soil and water.

To purify the atmosphere and heal the air in the room, send Reiki energy with both hands to every corner of the room, on the walls, floor, and ceiling.

If you want to "recharge" your food with Reiki energy, direct it to the ingredients before cooking or to cooked food before eating it. Keep your hands above the food or touch the dishes in which it lies with your hands and direct energy there.

As a matter of fact, you can apply the Reiki method daily in relation to any object - to medicines, perfumes, and even to your wallet. It takes a little time - just one moment, and the effect will be amazing.

Now, let's move directly to healing techniques.

Beesen

The Beesen technique is also called the "scanning technique." Translated from Japanese, the word "bee" means "treat," and the word" sen "means" determine," establish."

Activate the three energy centers.

Join hands in Gassho. Ask Reiki for energy to enter you and direct your hands to the part of the patient's body that needs treatment. Follow your feelings. If no sensations have arisen immediately, place your dominant hand on the patient's crown chakra.

If you still do not feel the "direction," slowly move your hands along the patient's body, from top to bottom and at a small distance. Feeling a tingling sensation in your hands, warmth, attraction, pressure, know that you have found the right place on the body. You will be able to see or hear the necessary information.

There is a feeling of unpleasant pain in the hands, rising to the elbows and even to the shoulders, at the moment when you reach the problem area of the patient. In this situation, you can't remove your hands; on the contrary, you need to continue to hold them until this sensation leaves your hands through your fingertips. After that, you can move them to another position. It is believed that this unpleasant sensation called "hibiki" (resonance) occurs when Reiki's positive energy is directed to a negatively charged area of the body.

With Beesen, sensations vary depending on the type and stage of the disease, as well as on the personality of the patient. Using the sensation of movement, pulsation, tingling, heat, or cold, you can determine the disease, its stage and the time required for healing.

In any case, each person has his own ailments (even if he is not aware of them), so you need to be very careful when performing Beesen technique. With this approach, you will be able to heal the disease before it manifests.

If, during the process of Reiki's influence, you got rid of the sensations of Beesen, then you prevented the disease.

The sensations of Beesen can be manifested not only in the problem area, but also in some other area: for example, with a disease of the stomach - in the forehead, and with problems with the liver - in the eyes, etc.

In general, the ability to beam in different people manifests itself in different ways. And if you do not rush, then you can develop this ability in yourself. You just need to give yourself time to get used to the sensations in your hands and thoughts. The best assistant in this process is your intuition.

The technique ends in the position of Gassho.

Gyoshi ho

Gyoshi ho's technique is called "eye healing." The Japanese word "gosh" means "sight." Dr. Usui argued that energy is emitted by all parts of the body, but especially by the hands, eyes, and breathing. And this technique teaches us to use the energy emitted from the eyes.

First, try to do this technique not with a person, but, for example, with a flower. Take the flower in your hand or place it two steps away from you, at eye level. Defocus your gaze and look through it. After some time, you will find that you can see almost 180 degrees.

Look at the flower and let the image come closer to you. Soon you will feel a very subtle form of breathing emanating from your eyes, associated with inhaling and exhaling. This exercise should be performed for 10 minutes every day until you understand that you can use your gaze to treat people.

Defocus your gaze. In other words, make sure that it is not intently in a stare. The fact is that in the gaze, there is certain aggression, and this is contraindicated for treatment.

Gently focus your eyes on the part of the body that you want to treat, and look there for several minutes. Then stop "actively" looking at your patient and let his image "enter your eyes." Notice how a circle of energy is created between you and the patient: its energy enters your eyes. You can put Reiki symbols on the part of the body that you want to treat.

If you liked this technique, you could also try Trataka meditation:

Sit back and look at a candle for 45-60 minutes. Try not to blink your eyes, even if after a few minutes they begin to watery. Keep your gaze on the candle. By practicing this technique regularly, you can safely perform it for an hour. Your consciousness will become like a laser beam - as sharp and focused.

Practicing with a candle can scare you: then do a Trataka meditation with a photograph or a lit statuette. You can do this while in a dark or dark room with your reflection in the mirror or with a person sitting opposite.

Affirmations

If you work with yourself, make affirmations - positive judgments. If you are working with a patient, help them compose affirmations. Affirmation should be short, accurate, and positive. It must be compiled in the present tense, in the words of the person who uses it, and in his native language. It is important that you do not limit it to anything. Of course, it will take time to understand what a person really wants in life. After all, our desires are not always obvious.

Activate the three energy centers.

Place the non-dominant hand (left, if you are right-handed) on the patient's forehead (or on your forehead), and the dominant one on the back of the head. Keep them like this for about 3 minutes, mentally repeating the composed affirmation. Then forget about affirmation, remove the non- dominant hand from your forehead, and simply give Reiki energy to the patient with the dominant hand lying on his head. Fold your hands in Gassho at the end of the exercise.

It is known that Dr. Usui used the five principles of Reiki and the verses of Emperor Meiji as affirmations. You can do the same.

Joshin Kokyu Ho

This technique is aimed at healing the Tanden. We have already said that the word "tanden" in Japanese means a place located two to three fingers below the navel. Thus, first, you need to correctly determine the location of the tanden.

Put your feet shoulder-width apart. Take a deep breath several times. Relax and think about something nice. Open your mouth a little. Hold your tongue against your palate and inhale through your nose. Exhale through the mouth, allowing the tongue to naturally lower. Bend your knees and focus on the lower abdomen. Take a few steps very slowly.

Suddenly, you will become aware of a point in the lower abdomen, two to three fingers below the navel: it is in this place that your life force lies.

You have found your tanden and now you can start the breathing technique of the Joshin Kokyu Ho.

Place one or both hands on the lower abdomen and breathe in the place you touch.

Activate the three Tributes.
Place one hand on the tanden and the other across from the back. Hold your hands until you feel the effect is achieved. Fold your palms in Gassho.

Joshin Kokyu Ho is used as the main technique for creating energy. This technique can also increase willpower - both yours and your patient.

Hishiryo
Hishiryo is a navel healing technique. Translated from Japanese, the word "hizo" means "navel."

Activate the three energy centers.
Bend the middle finger slightly and lay it on the navel, gently press down; when you feel the pulse, you can start the exercise.

Let Reiki energy flow through your middle finger into your belly button. Perform this exercise for 5–10 minutes while your pulse and energy are in harmony. If you want to use this technique to treat another person, first make sure that he does not mind that you touch his navel.

Perform the technique very gently. At the end, slowly and smoothly remove your finger from the navel. Fold your hands in Gassho, then open your eyes.

Ge Doku Ho

Ge Doku Ho is called a detoxification technique. The word "ge" in Japanese means "conclusion," and the word "doku" - "poison" or "toxins." Using this technique, you can remove toxins from both your body and the patient's body. Thanks to this, you can get rid of the side effects of drugs.

Activate the three Tributes.

Place one hand on the tanden and the other on the back. Stay in this position for about 30 minutes until you imagine that all the toxins have left your body (or the patient's body) through your feet to the ground.

Fold your palms in Gassho.

Hanshin Koketsu Ho

The Hanshin Koketsu Ho technique is aimed at purifying the blood. The word "hanshin" in Japanese means "half the body," and the word "koket" means "purification of blood." The technique is used to return the patient to planet Earth after healing; helps people with mental disabilities.

Activate the three energy centers.

Ask the patient to lie with their back and to bend the knees slightly.

Putting your left hand on his shoulder, use your right hand to move from the left shoulder to the right buttock, from the right shoulder to the left buttock

-       15 times.

Swipe down with two fingers of the right hand from the seventh cervical vertebra down to the third lumbar vertebra. Press on the third lumbar vertebra and slightly restrain movement. Do this 10 times.

Swipe with two hands from the spine to the sides, from top to bottom, 10- 15 times.

Fold your hands in Gassho.

Syu Chu Reiki
Syu Chu Reiki is a group Reiki concentration exercise. Translated from Japanese, "syu chu" means "concentrated." This technique is performed in a group.

Activate the three energy centers.
All members of the group send energy to one person, wishing him health and happiness. Participants practicing the first stage of Reiki put their hands directly on the patient, and those who practice the second and third stages use symbols. This exercise can only be done with an emotionally balanced person, as it can have a very powerful effect. If the group is large, the exercise should be performed for 1-2 minutes with each.

If the group is so large that there is no way for everyone to put their hands on the patient, form several rows. The first healers lay their hands on the patient, and those behind them lay their hands on their shoulders.

Finish the exercise in the Gassho position.

Chapter 10 Yoga Therapy

This chapter is special. Why? This is due to the fact that people often start to engage in some kind of technology or activity precisely because of health problems, and are limited to these goals. Such limits personal freedom by binding. In this chapter, the principles and basic mechanisms will be set forth, on the basis of which everyone will be able to build a sufficiently self-sufficient and holistic system of healing for himself

\-   and for others.

To begin with, we should remember that before the organism is living, it possesses really unlimited resources for restoration, it is important to properly distribute the efforts and do not leave any stone unturned.

Step one: create a goal and adjust the background

It has already been said about the need for a correct and clear goal-setting: the person must know what they want from it. Intuition will then help direct the hands and in which direction it should go. However, abstract efforts will lead to abstract results. Those resources that will be released during the practice should be directed to something specific. Otherwise, the effect will be evenly distributed across all organs and systems, especially without emphasizing any organ. You must form an extremely clear, lively, "convex" image that carries information in itself simultaneously for all senses.

Let's see what happens in the life of an ordinary, normal person over time. A person is born, being the owner of a conditionally defined health potential. From the first moment of life, he is exposed to environmental factors, often not the most favorable ("... from the moment of birth, a person's life turns into a continuous process of dying."). A body part peel when unintentionally struck against a stone, and any virus that enters the body, even if it does not cause a disease, every meal, every breath, every heartbeat, every disease is inevitable, step by step, brings a person closer to the natural finale - the body runs out of safety and starts inevitably collapse. This often happens because an ordinary person simply does not imagine what should be his body and how it should be felt "from the inside" in optimal condition. It turns out that a person lives on the resources of his body, often ineptly squandering the potential of vitality and health, allotted to him by nature.

In general, the aging process of the body and the mechanism of the development of the disease can be described as follows: under the influence of external factors, even with strong body resistance, there remain many adverse effects. "Malfunctions" gradually accumulate in the body, some defects in the work of first small groups - cells, and later organs and their systems that are increasingly diverting the body away from the optimal - that is, its normal working condition. The "specific gravity of errors" is accumulating in cells and tissues, and the processes of degeneration of tissues and organs begin. In fact, if you look at it, the majority of diseases are based on degenerative-dystrophic tissue changes: gradually, sections of a healthy organ become denser for one reason or another, their normal structure is replaced by dense tissues, respectively, the total percentage of healthy working cells decreases.

This can be very clearly explained by the example of heart diseases: all of them basically have impaired blood supply and myocardial trophism, as a result of which changes in the structure of the heart begin. This is especially clearly seen in heart attacks: dead tissue is replaced by a scar, which significantly reduces the contractility of the myocardium, against the background of this compaction, rhythm and conduction disturbances appear. Then the process begins to develop at an increasing rate. So, the body gradually degenerates. In fact, similar processes occur in the human mind: unused qualities - the structural organs of consciousness, gradually die out as unnecessary, the general structure of consciousness is simplified, becomes primitive and degenerates, reducing the set of functions to the minimum necessary. Consciousness gradually "condenses" loses mobility.

This process can be compensated by a clearly constructed intention uniting all levels and structures of a human being, aimed at creating the most powerful and clear image-state of oneself in an ideal form. This is a kind of matrix of our optimal state, on which our whole body, emotional sphere, and sphere of consciousness are built. It is necessary to constantly maintain and develop this state, constantly adding as many shades to it as possible, making it more and more real and alive. So, gradually, we will be able to learn not to lose our own energy in the process of life, but rather, gradually draw to our center - the force that we once lost.

Creating a Goal for the Whole Body
This is the stage of creating a holistic strategy for a further, more or less long period of life. Our task now is to note for ourselves our initial state. Keeping this in mind, we try to see ourselves from the side, noting all our weaknesses - the self-diagnosis system in our body always works, we just don't need to stop it from reporting all detected damages. The principle is simple: on our internal "virtual" screen, without straining and not

expecting anything, we try to see ourselves. The picture that we will see will give fairly clear information about the real state of our organs and systems.

To begin with, it is worth turning to the anatomical atlas in order to at least, in general terms, imagine where which organ is located and how it looks.

The next stage is the search for the image of the ideal state of the whole body as a whole. You can turn to childhood memories (in early childhood, as a rule, we are much closer to our ideal state, we just do not have time to find all that number of masks that now make up our "alien" roles and identities) or just come up with a new image of ourselves anew. When a lively and clear image is created, we "try it on ourselves," enter it. If this is really what we need, we will immediately feel it - we will be comfortable, and the world around us will seem more vibrant and rainbow. In any case, we try to revive the feeling of childhood; this alone will greatly stimulate recovery processes.

Take this as a rule: if the body "believes" you, your image, it completely reorganizes its functioning mode. For this, you just need to return to it more often and get used to your new state more and more.

The last step at this point is to replace the old image with a new one. We combine the picture of the old image and the new ideal state; we try to make it so that all the components of the old image: colors, sensations from the other senses organically transfer to a new image, reinforcing it, making it even more bright and convex. We do this as often as there is enough "survivability" of the old image - until it once completely disappears.

As a possible option, here is one of the options for restoring your optimal initial state of feeling like a child: imagine yourself as a small child. Look into his eyes. What will you see there? Perhaps it will be sadness, longing for love – perhaps a love for you? Take the child in your arms, hug him. Let him feel how much you love him. Promise him that you will always be near and will be able to help him if necessary. Now make this image very small and place it in your heart. Let it be there so that you can give is such necessary love. Pass this feeling through yourself; let it go outside. Let it begin to change your own life.

Creating a Goal for a Specific Organ

This stage is the stage of constructing tactical, less global goals. It is no different from the previous one, except that here we are rebuilding the ideal state matrix for the organ that we are currently interested in. Here we simply specify the task.

Optimal Background Tuning

The optimal background is that the psycho-emotional state in which the body will recover as efficiently as possible, which, in fact, will start the recovery processes in it, and the overall level of its energy, respectively, will be maximum. In many psycho-training systems, such a state is called the state of the winner or something similar. It is important that the maximum rise is felt in this state. Everyone has their own best way to enter this state, and perhaps the most difficult in the initial period is to learn how to create this state and then constantly maintain it. We are trying to use all possible and accessible methods for this: films, music or any technological techniques.

It's convenient to use the following as a possible technique for entering the "activated" state: we release attention, evenly distributing it throughout the body, try to feel how the whole body is drawn into the breathing process, how the pores on its surface open, tissues begin to come to life. If there are no such sensations right away, then we create them. It already exists in us; it is important to learn how to distinguish it from the general background and maximize it. We are looking in the space inside the body for the zone that is currently at the peak of its activity. When we enter it with our attention, there is a surge of strength and freshness.

We begin to breathe in this place, with each inhalation-exhalation, increasing the volume of this zone, we try to fill the entire body from within with this sensation, to impregnate all tissues and organs. We saturate with this sensation the part of the body that interests us, create in it a kind of epicenter of this sensation. We enter this state in the morning; we try to start with it every day. Now our task is not to lose this feeling, as far as possible we try to strengthen it even more.

This is the core of the entire recovery system; without this state, it is hardly possible to cause radical changes in the established distorted relations between organs and systems. Even if you do, in this case, the efficiency of such activities will be significantly lower.

Step two: optimize your lifestyle

Another necessary element on the path to health is the introduction of certain adjustments to the mode of life. One of the most basic elements related here is nutrition. So many worthwhile books have already been written on this subject, that it hardly makes sense to dwell on this issue in detail. In the most general terms, the following should be said:

We exclude all heavy proteins and fats of animal origin from our menu: meat, replacing it with soy and products from it, and minimize the use of butter, replacing it with ghee. Also, exclude coffee and black tea. These products are acceptable in rather "extreme" situations - during periods of severe cold, for example, when sufficiently tough external stimulants are needed.

Meals - only when the body insists on the need for it. We do not overeat, always leaving empty space in the stomach after eating, there should remain a feeling of slight hunger. In fact, with the relatively efficient operation of body systems, the amount of food needed is minimal. If you are a constitutional "meat-eater" - it happens, such people are basically not able to do without meat - we try, at least.

Food is not only a source of building materials for the body but also an element that irritates the immune system. In addition, each serving of food passing through the intestine has an effect on its walls, similar to the action of sandpaper - food masses desquamate the intestinal epithelium; this is necessary for normal digestion. That is, for the normal functioning of the same immune system or intestines, on the one hand, an influx of energy and "building materials" is necessary, and on the other, what we eat has a destructive effect on these systems. All body structures should be able to fully recover.

In addition, in the conditions of constant intake of nutrients, decay products that are not completely eliminated are constantly accumulated. All that was said is to justify the need to periodically arrange for yourself the so-called fasting days. This is not starvation; hunger for the body is a condition in which it is forced to break down its own tissues. A few days without food, under no circumstances, will lead to this.

There is always a certain amount of nutrients in the body - as if put aside "in reserve." These "stocks" must be periodically updated: products, even when stored in the refrigerator, deteriorate. A pause in food intake for 24-36 hours approximately once a week may well help. Traditionally, it is recommended in yogic literature to do such periods of "food abstinence" on the new moon, full moon, 11th, 26th, and 29th days of the lunar month. On such days, we drink little, but often: herbal infusions (if you used to drink herbs and you know which ones are right for you) or just green tea. If, for the first time, pesters hunger, the more we try to drink more often: water leaches the gastric juice, which in many ways causes hunger. However, gradually, the body will get used to it.

All of the above rules regarding the restructuring of the diet are the simplest elements in the recovery system, which, however, are amazingly effective. In just a week or two, you will notice how much the perception of yourself and your body has changed: it becomes more relaxed, flexible, obedient, and movement becomes easier and more pleasant, and perception becomes clearer and brighter. The severity and inertness gradually and imperceptibly disappear completely.

The optimal set of products for each person is different, if you want to rebuild your diet "as science says", you should turn to books on Ayurveda, although by and large it will be absolutely simple to pay attention to your own feelings about the time of eating, diet, quantity, etc. likewise, a simple understanding that all internal organs need to be cleaned of accumulated waste products over the time is necessary.

In addition to periodic "food abstinence," it is advisable to use special cleansing procedures, their technology has already been described many times in other books: from those devoted exclusively to healing to books entirely about yoga. In hatha yoga, importance is attached to techniques for cleaning the nose (neti), eyes (trataka), tongue, stomach, intestines (basti). However, before mastering these techniques, it is advisable to consult with an experienced yoga instructor.

By and large, there is no need to use all of them: it's worth choosing a few that are most suitable for the situation and use them regularly, when these organs are unloaded to some extent, the rest will become more active, and the effect will increase exponentially.

To facilitate the task of constantly maintaining an optimal state, we adhere to, at least the first time, a certain mode of life: we go to bed early, get up early, twice a day - water cleansing procedures (bathing). We avoid any negativity in relation to myself; as much as possible, we support the inner feeling of strength and self-determination, the state when you reach "I can achieve everything." As often as possible, if possible, several times a day, we actively load the body with physical exercises, without which, ideally, it should not receive food.

Step three: work with the body

Firstly, to constantly maintain the optimal level of activity of consciousness and the body, all the usual types of physical activity are necessary: swimming, running, etc. Secondly, specific activity is highly desirable: the so-called gymnastic part of yoga therapy, which, in many respects, determines its truly amazing effectiveness. Here at this point, it is worth stopping in more detail.

The practice of asanas in the therapeutic version makes it possible to work out all internal organs, activating the blood flow and nerve plexuses, leveling the hormonal and psycho-emotional background.

In general terms, this mechanism can be described as follows. Most of the diseases can be relatively arbitrarily characterized as a disruption in the functioning of the body systems, accompanied by a violation of blood flow in the tissues of various internal organs (vasoconstriction due to edema with inflammation or for other reasons) and a violation in the innervation of the affected organs. Several of the parts of the nervous system are responsible for this. Cells that have lost their normal energy levels partially or completely lost their functions, simply cannot recover in the absence of a full connection with the body and its regulatory systems. Accordingly, it is possible to restore the normal function of an organ by increasing the blood flow in it and activating the nearby nerve plexuses and higher sections of the nervous system.

The most important thing to remember during training is what you started to do. This has already been discussed in detail above. There must always be a clear awareness of the goal, its bright and strong image. When stretching the ligaments, the main principle of work is: we take a breath from those areas that are now "stretching" - from the joints and ligaments in which tension is felt, as if we are sucking it out, lifting it along the spine into the head, "impregnating" it with our image of ideal condition, and we return back, pumping joints and ligaments to the limit with breath.

In case of diseases of the abdominal organs, all asanas where the abdominal cavity is squeezed will be useful: by reducing its volume, intra-abdominal pressure rises, and blood from the aorta is squeezed out under increased pressure directly into all abdominal organs, activating metabolic processes in them and saturating the tissues with oxygen. This includes all the deflections and especially the deflections lying on the stomach, various twists, inclinations to one, and two legs from different positions, mayurasana, as well as all asanas, where the muscles and ligaments of the legs are actively stretched and the hip joints open.

Here it is necessary to carry nauli - band techniques, where work is actively used the front wall of the abdomen and all the breath at inhalation and exhalation, accompanied by bandhas (mula bandha, jalandhara bandha, and uddiyana bandha). All this works equally well for diseases of the liver, stomach and intestines, pancreas and kidneys, and pelvic organs. Also, in this situation, asanas will be useful in which the main load (stretching and tension) is on the legs and especially the hip joints. All standing asanas, all types of twine, butterflies, asanas with one or two legs under the arm, behind the head and all lotus elements are also effective.

In diseases accompanied by congestive processes in the organs (many diseases of the intestine, internal genital organs, etc.), all inverted elements will be very effective, especially all versions of the so-called "Egyptian" inclinations and twists, adding as much as possible to all inclinations during the fixation of the position of uddiyana bandha and nauli to strengthen the body.

For diseases of the organs of the chest cavity, it is worth using those exercises in which the chest is deformed, and the pressure in it increases accordingly. This group also includes, first of all, bends and all kinds of tilts to the sides, as well as those asanas where we are actively forced to use our hands and shoulder girdle. Dynamic practices will also be useful because of their training effects on the organs of the chest cavity. In inverted asanas, blood is redistributed and in the abdominal and chest cavities. There is a relative overflow of blood vessels, which also favorably affects the state of organs.

In the case of heart disease, one should be extremely careful and build up the load very gradually. In any case, we focus on well-being.

All bandhas affect the state of the chest organs. When working with them in this case, it is especially important not to pinch the chest, leaving its internal volume as free and straightened as possible.

For diseases of the visual and auditory apparatus, all inverted positions, as well as asanas where the cervical spine is pulled or twisted, will be useful. If the brain is pulled into the pathological process, one should work extremely carefully and, rather indirectly: the main impact is on other departments with the simplest exercises, and through the normalization of the main functions, the state of the brain is corrected. All bandhas used in pranayama also affect intracranial pressure.

In diseases of the spine, it is first necessary to restore the correct position of the vertebrae relative to each other. To do this, you first need to stretch the spine. For this purpose, it is convenient to use various forward bends, rolls on the back, asanas where the legs rest on the hands. However, the simplest option is the usual bakasana. Further, it is advisable to use twisting. Here, the possible set of these exercises is very large. After this, you need to strengthen, fix the newly rebuilt spine with a muscle corset. The possible and affordable set of asanas here is also very large: these are various face-ups with arms behind, and back deflections, which in themselves have a pronounced training and restorative effect on the intervertebral joints and stimulate the spinal cord, nerves, and plexuses adjacent to the spinal column, which is extremely beneficial for the condition of internal organs. Deflections, in turn, must be compensated by stretching the spine forward and twisting.

With spinal instability do not particularly zeal with stretches, so as not to stretch the intervertebral ligaments even more. Without a strong working muscle corset that fixes the spine, it will not be possible to fully restore it: the vertebrae simply will not be able to remain in an optimal position for a long time. The muscle corset is not only the back muscles, but also the oblique muscles of the abdomen and, in general, the muscles of the abdominal press. Accordingly, you should definitely include exercises for these muscle groups in your training. Such an approach will make it possible to deal with many problems, including severe injuries, in which surgical treatment or Reiki healing can be used. As the main principle of working with the spine, it is worth noting its constant stretching; any movement is made on a well-elongated spine, which should be followed in everyday life.

In general, it should be noted that many diseases of the internal organs are caused by just spinal problems.

In diseases of the joint-ligamentous apparatus of the extremities, it is especially necessary to carefully approach the development of damaged zones. If there is damage to the joint of a rheumatic nature or the type of osteoarthritis, when the joint surface is damaged, so as not to damage it, even more, do not immediately begin to actively load this joint. You need to start with tensile loads, and you need to select exercises so that there is no significant load on the body weight or stress on this joint.

If the joint or a group of joints are unstable, which sometimes happens after ruptures of the ligaments, or there is any other pathology associated with damage to the ligamentous apparatus, the approach should be the opposite: the joints should be actively loaded with power work, not really trying to stretch them at first. It is worth using both dynamic and static loads: this develops various groups of muscle fibers, and ligaments are strengthened more efficiently.

A sufficiently universal asana in this sense is a properly performed ordinary slide (uttan adho-mukha-svanasana). The technique of internal work in it has already been described above. The full practice of this asana in this version will make it possible to deal with problems of the spine, disorders in the central nervous system, organs of the chest and abdominal cavity, especially the lungs, heart, liver, kidneys, and in general the genitourinary system, joints and ligaments of the arms and legs. There is also a pronounced harmonizing effect on the endocrine glands. The effect can be enhanced by alternating a series of hyperventilation methods like kapalabhati or bhastrika with uddiyana bandha and nauli.

In diseases of the endocrine glands, all deflections tilts, and twists are very effective, especially those in which the main effect is on the spine at the level of the gland of interest to us. For the pancreas and adrenal glands, the same principles in work will be effective for other pelvic organs.

If there is a general weakness and lack of tone, hypotension, a tendency to depression, then it is necessary to focus on the practice of standing and power asanas, deflections mainly by the type of bridges and work in a dynamic mode. If the situation is the opposite

- there is a tendency to hypertension, emotional instability, with a feeling of general tension, then we focus on stretching asanas. It is better to do them on the floor, with long relaxing fixations in order to minimize stress.

In any case, the body sooner or later begins to prompt itself on when what, and how best to do. It is important to simply understand that the real master of the situation is you yourself, and take responsibility for everything that happens in your life for yourself.

As the effect increases, it is important not to stop there, but to constantly increase the load and the degree of complexity of the exercises. Thus, the body will be forced to constantly be in a state of complete mobilization, which will help to quickly return the lost power potential to the body.

At the end of each lesson, check the effectiveness of work. Again, as already described above, we are trying to see our body on the virtual screen, as if from the outside, tracking the changes in the "diagnostic" image that we managed to achieve. It is necessary to carry out the correction again, now the final one: again, we check the image obtained with the standard and try to remove all inconsistencies, maximizing the state that is our standard.

Thus, from time to time, step by step, rebuilding your body, re-creating ourselves as we want to see ourselves.

Chapter 11 Introduction to Meditation

Meditation has become more popular around the turn of the millennium, but it goes back thousands of years. The word meditation comes from the Latin word meditatum which means to ponder. It has been practiced in different forms throughout many different locations and traditions, but it originated in India between 5,000 and 3,500 BCE from evidence of temple and cave carvings. It was practiced first by the Vedic sages and cave yogis, with the first written evidence in the Vedas, a Hindu spiritual scripture, in 1,500 BCE after being passed down orally for centuries.

A Timeline of Meditation Development & History
The sages and yogis were the religious people who wandered around the Indian subcontinent as ascetics. Through the meditative practices, they were able to connect with universal forces and transcendental reality known as the creator of Brahman in the Vedic scriptures. From these texts, there have been hundreds of techniques and lineages of this information being shared through the generations.

It is thought that the original technique was through gazing or mantra meditation. Gazing is where a specific object is looked upon with intent whereas mantra meditation consists of a phrase of Sanskrit words which would create a specific sound and vibration depending on the purpose of the mantra. The modern movement of Yoga has basis in meditation along with breathing exercises coupled with postures and also originated in India.

Meditation continued to be practiced in the branch of Hinduism known as Buddhism. In the 6th century BCE, the prince known as Siddhartha Gautama renounced his royal life to live a life of an ascetic so that he could gain enlightenment. Through his journey, he learned philosophy and meditation techniques through the rishis, or sages. Throughout this process, he diverted from the Hindu traditions and created what is known as Buddhism today. He was successful in his goal of attaining enlightenment and became the Buddha. He then dedicated his life to teaching spiritual awakening and meditation. Over the course of decades, he was able to teach thousands of people.

In modern times, there are several lineages which have their own styles of meditation known as Walking Meditation, Loving-Kindness, Samatha and Vipassana.

These types of meditations spread to the West over the centuries, and are the most widely practiced forms of meditation today.

During the same time period of Buddha, there were three religions which were created that had their own teachings on meditation. These were Confucianism, Taoism and Jainism.

Confucianism centers around morality and community. Their form of meditation has a focus on self-improvement and self-contemplation, and is name Jing Zuo. Confucianism is still popular today, but is mainly found in Asia.

Taoism is focused on creating a union with the Tao, or cosmic nature and life. Their meditation technique helps with the generation, transformation and circulation of the energy within the body, known to them as Chi. This type of meditation aids in finding inner peace by unifying with the body, spirit and Tao and quietens the mind and body.

Jainism's meditation technique uses self-inquiry, visualizations, breath awareness, gazing and mantra repetition. Their religion is based on the ascetic lifestyle and focuses on non-violence, contemplation, self-discipline and self-purification.

The Greek philosophers of Aristotle and Plato developed their own technique of meditation through the influence of the yogis and sages of India. This happened during the time of Alexander the Great's military efforts in India between 327 – 325 BCE). Meditation was not the only influence to the Greek philosopher's system as they admired the sages' immunity to discomfort and pain and their particular disinterest in pleasure and their fearlessness of death.

The meditation technique that was created by the Greek philosophers was known as navel-gazing. This involves deep contemplation of a single issue of oneself. In later years, the philosophers Plotinus and Philo of Alexandria also created a type of meditation that focused on concentration. However, once Christianity started to dominate Europe, the influence of Eastern thought was abruptly cut. However, the ideas started to resurface during the 20th century when Europe and the East started to communicate once again.

The Christians started their own type of meditation which also involved repetition of a religious phrase or word, much like a mantra, and they also would sit in silent contemplation upon God. One method of meditation practiced by the Hesychasm Christians was known as the Jesus Prayer which was developed in Greece between the

10th and 14th centuries. It is believed that this tradition of Christians was in contact with the sufis and Indian sages which influenced their type of meditation.

During the 8th century, a school of Buddhism known as Zen was founded by an Indian-Persian monk by the name of Bodhidharma. He had traveled to China to teach meditation in which the lineage of Chan was born which was adapted by Vietnam, Japan and Korea. All of these versions of meditation were known as Zen which had a massive influence on the Chinese culture and Taoism. Because of the influence from a collective of countries and traditions, Zen meditation is quite unique.

The meditation technique is known as Zazen and is still a popular method of meditation in the West today. Some lineages of Zen also have a method of meditation by the name of Koans. In this type of meditation, the teachers as their students to ponder on a puzzle or riddle in the form of phrases, questions and stories to discover the greater truths about themselves and the world.

The tradition of the Islam Sufis date back as far as 1,400 years, and they were influenced as well by Indian traditions. Their forms of meditation include gazing, the use of mantras and focused breathing exercises. Their practices are designed to solidify their connection with Allah, or God, and also include a method in which they will whirl around in circles to create this effect. In fact, this whirling method is still used in Turkey today.

The esoteric Jewish tradition of the Kabbalah had also developed their own forms of meditation during the 11th century. Their methods include deep contemplation of prayers, symbols, names of God and philosophical principles. They also would reflect upon the principle of the Tree of Life which is a representation of individual beauty, uniqueness and personal development. Similar to a tree, the branches growing up to the sky is a symbol of an individual becoming stronger as they strive for new experiences, wisdom and greater knowledge.

During the 16th century, the Eastern traditions were beginning to be translated into Western languages. The scriptures that were translated were the Buddhist Sutras, the Bhagavad Gita and the Upanishads. Two centuries later, Buddhist was a study for the intellectuals in the West with the philosopher Schopenhauer being one of the biggest admirers of the Eastern traditions and teachings. With the Transcendentalist movement in the United States, Henry David Thoreau and Ralph Waldo Emerson had deep ties to Eastern spirituality and philosophy.

During the 20th century, Swami Vivekananda had come to the United States to introduce meditation and yoga teachings. His debut of his philosophy was presented at the Parliament of Religions which took place in Chicago in 1893. This sparked great interest in the practice of meditation and was supported by the Transcendentalist movement as well. As a result, many well-known Indian babas, or teachers, moved to the United States like Swami Rama, Maharishi Mahesh Yogi and Paramahansa Yogananda to teach their methods of meditation. The Buddhists teachers also made their way to the United States teaching Tibetan, Theravada and Zen meditation.

Due to the influx and availability of Eastern teachings, the masters were able to create a large following which laid the groundwork to the ancient traditions to be taught and practiced today. This movement was furthered due to scientific studies being released that showed that mediation practices benefited those who were not specifically seeking spiritual enlightenment. For those who were not wanting to meditate for spiritual reasons, the teachings had to be modified to remove the spiritual context. Also, the practices were adapted for the Western way of life to be simpler as most of the western disciples would not be able to follow the strict guidelines which are found in the East.

During the 20th century, scientific studies on meditation started to emerge. The first tests were conducted in 1936 and the first collection of these studies were published in 1977 by James Funderburk who was a follower of Swami Rama. In fact, Swami Rama was the first of the Indian yogis who agreed to be studied by Western scientists. These tests were conducted in the 1960s where the yogi performed different practices such as voluntarily controlling his body temperature, blood pressure and heartbeat. Before these tests were conducted, it was believed that these were involuntary actions of the body. Due to these discoveries, scientists had interests in researching meditation even further.

Over the course of the next five decades, meditation has been extensively researched. With the advances in technology, the scientists were able to dig deeper to discover other benefits that meditation can have for the mind and body. Monks and llamas from the Zen and Tibetan traditions had been also studied which demonstrated the results of mind-over-body practices. During the early years of the 1970s, Dr. Herbert Benson of Harvard University created a major shift in the thought that meditation was solely for religious purposes. Through his research, he was able to show that meditation could be used for healthcare purposes as well.

As a result, meditation during the 21st century has become widely popular and secularized. There are still spiritual meditation practices which are used today in the Western countries, but most use the secular approach to realize the benefits to the overall wellness of the mind and body. The people who meditate regularly report they have positive changes in the mental and physical wellbeing in their lives as well as having a more peaceful and calmer outlook.

The Basics of Meditation

There are many different types of meditation, but they are all based upon the same basic principles. Before you start your meditation practices, you need to prepare yourself so that you are able to get the most out of your time.

Preparing for Meditation

Following these basic steps are going to help ease you into your meditation practice.

❖ Find a place which you are going to be comfortable sitting. It does not need to be completely quiet as a small amount of background noise will be fine.

❖ Wear clothing that you feel relaxed and comfortable in. If you are wearing constrictive clothing such as a scarf, belt or tie, you likely will want to loosen these ahead of time. If you are wearing shoes that are tight or heels, you will need to remove them.

❖ Whether you decide to lay down or sit in a chair, you want to have

your back straight, your chin tucked in slightly and your neck muscles relaxed. You can place your hands where they feel comfortable on your knees or your lap if you are sitting. When laying down, you can lay your hands next to your body or fold them over your stomach or chest.

❖ Choose a time that you will be able to perform meditation each

day by coupling it with a concrete routine such as brushing your teeth. Getting yourself in the habit of spending time in quiet contemplation will create a ripple effect of benefits in your life.

❖ Knowing your purpose and intention of wanting to incorporate a

meditation practice in your life will help drive you. If you know what your motivation is to practice, you will be more likely to build your habit of practicing meditation.

❖   There is no such thing as a good or bad meditation. There are

going to be some days you will not connect with the passing thoughts in your mind and others where you cannot stop engaging.

This is okay. Be kind and remind yourself that this practice is to ultimately teach you patience. Continue the next day with a clean slate and do not stop because you think you are doing it wrong. It simply is not true. Over time you will find that your mind will be less distracted with thoughts and the process will be much simpler.

Basic Meditation Exercises

There are several approaches that one can take when wanting to incorporate a meditation practice. Try the following exercises to see which one works best for you personally.

Mindfulness Meditation Exercise

This type of meditation is going to strengthen your mindfulness and attention. It will help you to stay present in this given moment and anchor yourself in your purpose without judgement in the here and now.

Step 1: Lie or sit down in a comfortable position. This can be on the floor or in a chair. If you are sitting in a chair, be sure to have your feet flat on the ground during meditation. If you choose to sit on the floor, you can make yourself more comfortable with a meditation cushion or yoga mat. You can sit in a cross-legged position or sitting on your bent legs. Whatever position you choose, you need to be comfortable during the entire meditation.

Step 2: Close your eyes and breathe naturally.

Step 3: While you are breathing, take notice of the movement of the body with each inhalation and exhalation. Focus on your belly, rib cage, shoulders and chest movements. Continue to breathe naturally during this process. If your mind should wander, bring your focus back on your breathing.

Step 4: Continue this practice between two and three minutes if you have never practiced meditation before. Build up the time each day to a time frame which you are comfortable.

Step 5: Slowly open your eyes and take your time moving.

There is no set time you must meditate, but it is helpful if you are able to quiet your mind for a minimum of 15 minutes each day. You will want to perform your meditation practice at the same time each day. Continuing to focus on your breathing will help to clear your mind. Once you master this technique, you will be able to perform other types of meditation with ease.

Evaluate your Meditation Practice

Especially when you are beginning with your meditation practices, it is important to evaluate when you had learned during the meditation practice. Ask yourself the following questions:

❖ How many breaths did it take before your mind wandered away from focusing on your breathing?

❖ Did you take note of how much busier your mind was, even when you were trying to clear your mind?

❖ Were you getting caught up in your thoughts when this occurred?

Knowing the answers to these questions will give you deeper insight as to how your mind goes about its daily tasks. It also shows you that the mind can be overworked and full of nonsense that can take you away from focusing on what is important. Know that you are not alone. These thoughts racing through your mind is the product of not being present in the current moment, and we have grown comfortable in allowing our thoughts take over our brains.

Practicing meditation helps to calm down this freight train of thoughts and allows you to recognize these thoughts as passing ideas. Being able to see your thoughts in a different perspective will allow you to not have to become involved in every thought that comes up in your mind. They simply come and go, and the more that you practice meditation, the more the thoughts and mind will calm down.

Remedying Common Mistakes for Meditation Practice

When you are just starting out, there are many obstacles that you can create which will hinder your confidence or progress with your meditation routine. Let us go over several common ways that you are cutting yourself short from your true potential of your meditations and how to remedy or avoid them in the first place.

It is common as a beginner to feel an array of feelings such as resistant, overwhelmed, anxious, fearful, bored, restless or a combination thereof. Once you get over these initial feelings, you will notice them quickly vanish away. Remember, your mind is used to being busy all of the time. You are trying to improve that by slowing down your thought processes, and it is a result that will come with time.

You are able to help these initial thoughts by keeping to your scheduled time for meditation. There should be no excuses, and you always can make the time to sit in silence for 10 or 15 minutes a day. Doing something out of the norm can bring about these feelings, but put them aside just for these few minutes a day, and you will notice that they will not continue to come up before you meditation practice.

If you are not able to practice every single day, do not beat yourself up. Of course, you are going to find the benefits of meditation much more quickly practicing each day. However, the most important thing for beginners to realize is that they are taking baby steps in creating a new habit. The time you are able to dedicate to meditation, the more you are going to get out of it, but this does not mean that you must stress yourself out in the process.

Bottom line is, you need to listen to your body. If you are in a state of stress and being overwhelmed, you are very likely going to benefit from taking the time to meditate. Setting a time 2 to 3 times a week even will be more of a benefit if you waited, let us say a month, in between meditation sessions.

Feeling sleepy is another common issue to where you may even be nodding off during your meditation. This is a very common theme for beginners. When your mind is so used to being on the go, it can confuse your stillness with relaxation, causing you to feel more tired. After you continue the meditation practices, you will start to rewire your brain so that it understands you are not resting because you want to sleep.

Three ways that you are able to help this situation is to open a window so that there is a breeze in your meditation room. You can also set your meditation time during the morning or when your mind is more alert. If you are laying down, sit up during your meditation times.

Sometimes you may find yourself expecting too much too soon from your meditation practice. Letting go of your expectations and what you should expect to happen. Simply go with the flow of where your meditation exercises take you. Find enjoyment in how you feel when you are preparing, during and after your practice. Keep a journal of your journey as you continue through the meditation so that you are able to gauge what benefits you are seeing. Find happiness in the new way that you are living your life.

When you are just beginning with meditation, it is easy to believe that you must have complete silence. However, this is not the case. In fact, if you start your meditation practices in complete silence, you will find that you are going to get distracted very easily by outside noises that you cannot control.

Instead, be more concerned with finding a space that you are comfortable. When the sounds in your environment come up randomly, treat them like you thoughts, notice them and do not get involved. It does take some practice. Over time, you will be able to hear noises during your meditation and not be distracted away from your breathing. If you are having an especially difficult time concentrating, you can use noise canceling headphones, but you will need to eventually work your way to meditating when there is background noise.

Letting go of the stereotype that meditation is only for spiritual people, a new age idea or for tree huggers. In fact, there are people from all walks of life and age young and old who practice meditation. Of course, it can have a religious focus, but this is not necessary for meditation practice. Another misconception is that is has to be a serious matter with saying mantras of "om" and sitting cross legged. This is an idea that can be incorporated if you wish, but it is not necessary. So perform your meditation practice how you feel comfortable, no matter if you are 2 or 102 years old.

It can be an easy task to start something new because it can be an exciting experience. However, the trick is sticking with it when the novelty wears off. This happens because many of the meditation practices can feel repetitive. Remind yourself that you are training your mind to shift perspective on the way that you view your feelings and thoughts.

One main reason why people throw in the towel is that they do not feel like their mind is clear or empty. It simply is not working! However, like with all things that are worth achieving, there is a level of dedication and perseverance that is required so that you can push past this phase. Remember that the mind is programmed to think. Meditation is not a magical potion so that it will make your thoughts disappear completely. However, you need to learn, practice and master meditation, and the only way you are able to achieve this is to continue to build your habit of meditation.

Some are very excited about trying out a different technique each time they sit down to meditate. This is alright for a short time as you are beginning and finding the technique that resonates best with you. However, if you are continuously switching between methods, you are not going to gain the full benefits of the particular meditation you are performing.

Above all, make your meditation practice a part of your day that you look forward to. It is your way of keeping your mind balanced throughout the rest of the day, and you will help to keep you more focused and aware. Trust me, when you are able to keep up with your practices, you will start to see the benefits that ripple throughout your life. Then you will be wanting to share this secret with everyone.

Chapter 12 Introduction to Reiki

Reiki is an ancient technique which was created in Japan which centers around healing, stress reduction and relaxation. It is derived from two Japanese words. Rei means higher power where Ki has the meaning of life force energy. In full, the word Reiki means spiritually guided life force energy.

You practice Reiki methods by hovering your hands or lightly laying your hands in a particular area of the body to promote healing. It manipulates and transmutes the energy that is found within the body known as Chi, Shakti or Life Force. You are able to build energy if it is too low and lower it if it should be too high.

Reiki does not just revolve around the energies within the body. It has an effect on you as an entire person, encompassing the spirit, mind, emotions and the body in the treatment. You may find many benefits such as overall well-being, security, peace and relaxation. In some instances, there are people who experience miraculous results. Any individual is able to use Reiki because it is not based on spiritual development of intellectual capacity.

Even though Reiki is spiritually based, it is not a religion. There is no dogma attached and you do not need to hold particular beliefs to use Reiki. In fact, Reiki will work even if you do not have a belief in the practice itself, although, it would be more powerful if you do believe that it will work for you.

Using the techniques and intention of Reiki to heal and balance your body, you will be able to help your body to heal from different illnesses. It is believed that energy is blocked and cannot flow properly resulting in illness. When this blockage is removed, you will be able to treat the illness in a more direct way than with conventional medicine. You will find with the chakra meditations that you are able to utilize this transfer of energy to heal your energy centers of the body, resulting in lasting effects felt throughout your body on a physical, mental and spiritual level.

Health Benefits of Reiki

Overall, Reiki manipulates the movement of the life force energy within the body. You will be able to realize many physical and emotional benefits to include the following:

aids relaxation

assists in the natural healing process

hightens spiritual, mental and emotional well-being helps with coping with difficulties

relieves emotional stress

From a medical standpoint, Reiki has been successfully used to treat and sometimes cure:

Fatigue syndromes Crohn's disease

Autism

Neurodegenerative disorders Infertility

Chronic pain Depression Anxiety

Heart Disease Cancer

Stress

Reiki Healing for Anxiety & Stress

Anxiety and Stress are the most experienced medical conditions which are seen in modern society. Reiki healing can be a huge benefit to relieving the symptoms of these experiences. Let us go over the basics of these two conditions so that you can realize if you have problems with them and how reiki and meditation can help you in these cases.

Anxiety

Having occasional experiences of anxiety is a normal fact of life. However, if you are having issues with anxiety that are affecting your daily life, this is known as an anxiety disorder. This is where you are experiencing frequent amounts of persistent and excessive worry which is intense. They can involve repeated occurrence of sudden feelings, and they can also result in panic attacks which are fear, torror and intense anxiety about a particular situation.

These anxiety disorders can start to develop as early as childhood or teenage years and continue to strengthen in intensity during your adulthood. You may start to revolve your day avoid particular places or people so that you do not trigger your emotions. The common disorders of anxiety are known as generalized anxiety disorder, social anxiety disorder and separation anxiety disorder. You are able to have two of these anxiety orders simultaneously.

Common Symptoms of Anxiety

From the wide range of anxiety disorders, the most common symptoms are:

difficulty controlling worry – this is the symptom experienced the most. It is categorized by the worry being disproportionate to the situations that trigger the worry. Usually, it is connected with everyday situations.

To be diagnosed with generalized anxiety disorder, you must have frequent occurrences of uncontrollable worry over the course of six months.

difficulty sleeping – Disturbances in sleep are highly associated with anxiety disorders. This can include a wide range such as waking up in the middle of the night, difficulty falling asleep and insomnia. It is unclear what the link is between anxiety and sleeping disorders. However, when the anxiety disorder is treated and under control, the sleep issues improve as well.

trouble with concentration – This is a heavy hitter when it comes to anxiety disorders. More than 2/3 percent of the people suffering from anxiety disorders have issues with focus, short term memory and concentration. Even with this large number, it is not a surefire way of knowing you have issues with anxiety.

overactive or feeling tired – Even though this can be a symptom for a wide range of disorders, becoming easily fatigued is a red flag for doctors when discussing anxiety disorders. Because of this reason, this symptom alone is not able to lead a doctor to a diagnosis of anxiety disorder. Alternatively, you can also experience the opposite of having hyperactivity. Fatigue is trickier as it can be an occurrence experienced only after panic attacks or it can be chronic and experienced throughout the day.

hyperventilation or rapid breathing – Panic attacks happen when you are under an immense amount of worry, and this leads to you not being able to physically be able to breath without hyperventilating. It is due to an intense amount of fear and can be a debilitating experience. Panic attacks usually have fear of dying, nausea, chest tightness, shaking and sweating that occur with the rapid breathing. They must occur frequently to be deemed as worthy of a diagnosis.

Feeling agitated – When anxiety hits a person, their sympathetic nervous system is sent into overdrive. With this effect, it causes a ripple effect throughout the body, resulting in symptoms of dry mouth, shaky hands, sweaty palms and a racing heart. This is in response to your brain believing that you are in danger overall feeling of tension, restlessness or nervousness – This is a symptom seen mainly in teens and children. It is categorized by the individual feeling like they are on edge or experiencing an uncomfortable urge to move. Even though it is a symptom that is not found in each patient, it is one of the indicating symptoms that doctors look for before diagnosis.

Causes of Anxiety Disorders

There are many causes of anxiety disorders that are not fully understood because it affects each individual on a personal level. Traumatic life experiences are going to affect people in different ways. It is thought that inherited personality traits may also be a cause of people being more sensitive to anxiety issues.

For others, underlying medical issues can be to blame as the cause for anxiety disorders. In fact, seeing signs of anxiety usually triggers an investigation which brings these medical conditions to light. Here is a list of common medical issues which are seen in conjunction with anxiety disorders.

Chronic pain

Irritable bowel syndrome

Withdrawal from medications or alcohol Misuse of drug or withdrawal

COPD or asthma Hyperthyroidism Diabetes

Heart disease

You can also be at increased risk of having an anxiety disorder if you have issues with one or more of the following:

Alcohol or drugs

Having a family history of anxiety disorders in blood relatives' Other mental health disorders such as depression

Buildup of stress due to illness or a death in the family Trauma

Stress

Stress is very common today, and it is an emotional or physical response to pressures or demands that are experienced daily. Stress can be a positive part of life when experienced in small doses. It is able to help people to take action, be stimulated, develop and to grow. However, if you are experiencing high levels of stress frequently, it can be due to an imbalance in lifestyle and can include any area of your life such as illness, relationships, money and/or work.

Common Symptoms of Stress

When you having issues with prolonged stress, your symptoms can include one or more of the following:

Irritability

Difficulty with making decisions Difficulty relaxing

Depression

Lowered confidence levels Difficulty concentrating Sleep disturbances

Difficulty breathing

Decreased sexual function or libido Appetite changes

Muscle spasms or nervous twitches Headaches

Low energy levels

Muscle pain and spasms High blood pressure

Hyperventilation Heart palpitations

Gastrointestinal issues such as irritable bowel syndrome, heartburn and indigestion

Anxiety

Autoimmune diseases Withdrawal from others

Procrastinating or neglecting responsibilities

Causes of Stress

There are many levels of causes which can lead to stress. Most of them are extreme changes to our normal day routine. External causes of stress include the following:

Children and family members Having too busy of a schedule Financial issues

Romantic relationship difficulties School or work

Major life changes

Internal causes of stress are the following:

All or nothing attitude

Perfectionism or unrealistic expectations Negative self-talk

Lack of flexibility or rigid thinking Inability to accept uncertainty Pessimism

The most common life events which can cause undue stress are the following:

Retirement

Marriage reconciliation Job loss

Marriage Illness or injury

Death of a close family member Imprisonment

Separation in a romantic relationship Divorce

Death of a spouse or partner

These causes can lead to results or symptoms in our life that rise in a physical way. Some examples are:

-       acne – This is likely the most visible way that stress reveils itself. This is due to people touching their face more often when they are stressed which leads to the spread of bacteria and the appearance of acne.

- headaches – Stress can lead to pain within the head as well as the neck. This happens in over 50% of people who experience undue stress in their lives. The pain can range in intensity and can even be debilitating.

- frequent illness – Having heightened levels of stress lowers the immune system effectiveness leading you to feel sick more often than if you did not have undue stress in your life. This leads to illnesses ranging from a runny nose to the flu. However, be sure to look at your physical exercises level and your diet to see if they are to blame first.

How Reiki Can Help

In general, Reiki helps a person to feel more calm and centered. They are able to take back control of their lives without the use of expensive doctors and treatments. In fact, you are able to use these tactics yourself, so you can heal your body when you feel out of balance. Being able to use the healing energy work of Reiki helps own to feel more in control and more confident.

Anxiety and stress symptoms are able to be dealt with on a personal level which is unique to the individual. Since both of these diagnosis stems from personal perspectives on life's events, it is important to approach the healing in a very personal way. Reiki and meditation are able to help you do just that.

As for the physical symptoms that can be experienced, being able to calm down the and make the energy flow properly throughout your body, the ripple effect is going to come down to changes in your body physically. Many of the physical symptoms of stress and anxiety are going to be erased due to the correct energy flow.

Being able to balance out the energy flowing through your chakras, it also reduces the response from the brain to go into flight or fight mode. When you are more calm and centered, you will be able to think more clearly and feel more vibrant.

In fact, more and more private practices, hospice and hospitals are incorporating Reiki sessions coupled with modern medicine. There have been many patients who have reported that they had a reduction in their symptoms, which makes it a beneficial approach to those suffering from anxiety and stress.

So Why 21 Days of Reiki?

There is an intense amount of cleansing that is occurring in the body during this process of healing. You need to ensure that you are drinking enough water and getting a sufficient amount of sleep so that your body is able to cleanse more efficiently. When you work with the meditations, you are also going to be clearing out negative energies and toxins that have built up over your lifetime. There are 7 main chakras which are worked with, and each chakra has 3 days of practice.

With the amount of new energy that is being channeled into the body, it takes a course of 21 days for your body to adjust and adapt to the new activity. From a psychological standpoint, it takes approximately 21 days for a person to form a new habit.

Even though stress is put upon the first 21 days of starting Reiki, this does not mean that the process is complete after this time. It is very important to keep up the practices so that you able to reap the best results from practicing Reiki.

Continuing to practice daily is a way to ensure that you do not have a buildup of germs, emotions, negative thoughts or negativity in your life. You do not realize how much of these you pick up on a subconscious level each day. Being able to address these issues on a daily basis helps keep them at a minimum while you are reaping the benefits of living a balanced and healthy life.

Not only does daily practice keep these aspects in balance, it helps you to build up energy that has been lost throughout the day. As you continue the practice, you will continue to clear out your chakras which will lead you to see the full benefits of Reiki practice over time.

Even though this book focuses on the first 21 days, it is important to keep up the practice for a minimum of 3 months so that you can see the true effects that the Reiki has on your body, mind and spirit.

Chapter 13 Introduction to Psychic Abilities

Even though you may be unaware, every person is capable of tapping into their psychic abilities. This is because we are all immortal and infinite beings of energy and is comprised of a part of the universe

known as your soul. Most of us have been conditioned to believe that intuitive and psychic abilities are not actually true because there are many charlatans out there that take advantage of people with their "powers" better known as deceptions. Using a trick of the mind for people who are desperate or in need is a powerful tool that they are able to use to their own advantage. Because of the encounters with these people in the media or in real life, society as a whole are sceptical of psychic ability's existence.

A good example is when you were a child, you may have had more psychic encounters. Children are more in touch with the energies around them, and they are purer from the experiences of life. As a result, you likely were able to hear, dream or sense otherworldly energies or words. Because society has been conditioned to believe that psychic connections are not real, the adults in your life likely shrugged off your experiences or explained them away in a logical fashion.

However, there are some people who are fortunate enough to be able to learn about these abilities from their family members or other caretakers. These are the people that have a solid belief that there are other energies that exist outside of ourselves, and they will support and teach the connected child so that they are better equipped to deal with all of the rare occurrences that most people will consider them crazy.

As an example, you may have had an experience with communicating with a spirit or ghost who was not there in physical form, but you were able to see and play with them as if they were real. If you confide in your parents about this person, they likely were not able to see this spirit themselves, so instead of taking you at your word, they explain it by saying that you have an imaginary friend. This is a more accepted belief in society, although farfetched for some, but most people will not think the child is crazy for making up a friend to spend their time with.

Because this experience was not defined in the proper way, you yourself most likely started to believe that this spirit was all part of your imagination as well – that you created it in your mind. However, it is very likely that you were able to see what other people could not see because of your innocence and overall trusting of the world. The magic that is experienced in the world through the eyes of a child is lost usually as you get older and start to get bogged down with tragic and emotional occurrences ranging from love to working at a job. These are not part of a child's life, and therefore, their soul is cleaner for these higher energies to come through more easily.

Even if you have lost this connection as you become an adult, this does not mean this skill is forever lost. In fact, any person of any age is able to practice and work to strengthen their psychic abilities, and it requires an ample amount of self-love, exercise and patience. One of the main ways to achieve this is to switch your perspective that these abilities are a form of deception or falsehood. They are nothing of the sort, and you do not need to rely on what society has conditioned you to think through the media.

When you tap into your psychic skills, you are going to have heightened sensitivity to one or a combination of your taste, sense, feeling, hearing, vision and intuition of the energetic world. In fact in the science of psychology, there is no true definition as to how to define "normal" and as such, it is a personal scale that you base this upon. With these heightened perceptions, there are many levels of intensities. As you begin to get back in touch with your intuition and psychic abilities, you will find that the intensity will strengthen the more that you practice.

It is important to mention since you will be perceiving the world from a different perspective that you may feel more alienated as you will not be able to talk to just anybody about your personal experiences. However, there are many people just like you who have been practicing for various amounts of time that you will be able to confide in and even receive insight or guidance. Being able to tap into these extra sensory sides of ourselves, you will gain a better understanding of yourself and the world around you. The deeper you go, the most surreal your experiences to the point where you may find it difficult to put them into words. This is all part of the experience as you deepen your connection with yourself and the energies of the other worlds.

Connecting with your Intuition Again

When you are starting to work on your psychic abilities, it is imperative that you have a bond with your intuition. This relationship is going to strengthen and deepen over time as you learn to trust and truly listen to what your senses are telling you. You will start to notice the messages that your body is giving you through your intuition when you know the signs. You will need to pay close attention as we can hear a voice in our minds that we label as intuition, but it can be your ego trying to trick you that it is okay to do what you ultimately wanted to do in the first place.

One way to practice getting back in touch or strengthening your intuition is to create a visualization. See yourself a coffee shop sharing a drink with an old childhood friend that you have not seen since you were a child. You take the time to catch up on your experiences and go over all of the old stories that you shared together during your childhood. Through these conversations, you are able to remember the dynamic of the personal relationship that you had with them all this time ago, but it feels as if you had not spent so much time apart.

Even so, you feel a distance because of your different experiences you both have had and feel that you are strangers in this regard. To be able to take away this feeling of alienation, you would need to get to know your friend again as they are now instead of who they were in your memory.

This is the same way that you need to approach your intuition as if it was your old childhood friend. In this perspective, you are able to see that your intuition has always been a part of you, but you may have taken different routes and not kept in touch. However, it is always possible to rekindle this relationship with your intuition once again. Being able to take the time each day to work on this relationship just like you would with any other person, you will find that you will be able to cultivate this connection is a very personal way.

Intuition Building Exercises

To perform this exercise, you will need to evaluate your emotions and associate a color with each emotion. You can use the typical color representations such as blue meaning healing energy or red meaning angry. However, you need to pick a color scheme that resonates best with you for this exercise.

Start this practice by thinking of a situation which is straightforward, such as a text message with a potential partner or lover. You may have thoughts of love or disdain for this person. Depending on your personal feelings about this situation, assign a color to the feelings of love or disdain which may be pink or red for love and a more negative color such as black or purple for disdain. Remember there is no wrong color choice and you must choose the color that you personally would associate with your feelings.

During future interactions with this emotion and person, you will start to rewire your energy to associate this color with this particular emotion. Through this exercise, you will be able to strengthen your intuition by the color association and you will be able to communicate with your intuition nonverbally through these emotion-based colors. Over time, your intuition is going to be more in tune with these color schemes and be able to signal to you through colors so that you can see the bigger picture of a situation.

As an example, if you associated love with red, when your friend is talking about a specific person, and you are able to see the color red while she is talking about them, you will intuitively know that there is a loving connection between the two without your friend needing to express this directly.

Another practice is scanning a room so that you are able to get a feel for your current environment. This is done while you have positioned yourself in the center of a room which does not have other people there. You can choose to move around the energy of the space through the movement of your eyes to witness what is going on or you can physically move about the room. Take mental notes of the scents, sounds and sights that you are taking in. Ask yourself where you are being pulled to energetically and people and places that you feel like you should avoid. Be as detailed as possible by examining the furniture, windows and corners of this space and how they make you feel internally.

The more that you practice this exercise, you will be able to do this same practice in a room of people. This is a more intense version of the exercise, and may be intense the first time depending on your level of sensitivity. Listen to your body and cease if it should become too much. However, do not let these feelings of anxiousness divert you from developing your skills. There are going to be growing pains and tests along the way, but once you push through these feelings, great benefits await you on the other side.

You can also use this exercise in other places such as subways, offices, bars and parks. Being able to practice this technique in common areas that you frequent will help you to become more familiar with the energies of your surrounds and continue to solidify your relationship with your intuition.

Another exercise that you can practice is using the subconscious and your dreams. It is through your dreams that you are able to digest and absorb the energies that you come in contact with during the day that have not been particularly resolved. Since we are not able to live balanced and healthy lives by absorbing every instance that we encounter in a single day, our psyche comes into play to help us to find that balance that is required for a functional and healthy lifestyle.

Through dream work, you are able to remove the constraints of this physical plane where you are able to effortlessly move throughout spaces and other planes. It is rather common to encounter spirits of other realms, travel into the future as well as the past or explore foreign lands. There is no limit to where you can go in the subconscious which makes it an endless pool of possibilities to discover.

To be able to get the most of the knowledge that you gain through your dreams, be sure to keep a journal and pen next to your bed. It is all too common that you forget these adventures and information gathered in the dream world. You can curb this tendency by creating a habit of writing down what you remember the moment that you wake. This way it is fresh in your mind. Even if you only remember one part of your dream, write it down. You may find that you are able to remember other parts of your dreams as you writing down the one part that you remembered upon waking.

This is a daily practice which can also be used throughout the day. Strengthening your intuition requires that you are mindful of the people you surround yourself with. Make sure that you trust the people who are in your inner circle and that they are positive minded. Eliminate energy vampires out of your life if at all possible. Notice your levels of intuition while you are around certain people. If it is being strengthen while interacting with them, spend more time with them whenever possible. Guard the strength of your intuition by steering away from people who drain you, especially as you are working on building your skill.

Test your intuitive skills with your close friends by asking them about specific tips and information in which you are receiving. This will help guide you to trust your intuitive skills more when they confirm that your feelings and sensitivities are correct. As you deepen your trust in your intuition, you will learn to rely on it more fully and in effect it will strengthen.

Now that you have the basis to help you out with your daily self-care measures, you will be more ready to take on the challenges of fortifying your intuitive skills. Let us explore the other ways that you can strengthen your personal talents.

Set Challenges for Yourself

Set personal goals for yourself to continue to push yourself to your limits. Think outside of the box and expand your personal talents. This does not have to include sensitive matters. Examples include learning a foreign language, taking up a new hobby or even learning how to play a musical instrument.

This will continue to broaden your horizons, help you to come in contact with different types of people and strengthen your body and mind. This is turn will help you with your intuitive talents as you will be utilizing them to learn new things. You will also be humbled as you continue to learn and hone your skills. When you are in a humbled state, you become more empathetic and grateful.

While you are in position of challenge, these are times where you will learn more about yourself and how you interact with the world around you. You will grow in ways that you would not have without the challenge in place and end up being grateful for the experiences.

Get out of Your Comfort Zone

When you are put into new situations, it makes you rely more on your intuitive skills to help you navigate through unknown areas. Travel is especially a great way in doing this. Not only will you learn about new places, but you will come in contact with different cultures than your own. This will help to broaden your ideas and thoughts.

It will also help you to understand more types of people which will come in handy as it will aid you in helping different kinds of people. Gratefulness for the uniqueness of people will arise. Your listening skills will also be honed as you learn more about the new places and people. When you are forced to see situations in a different light, it sparks your creativity to find a solution to situations. This may help to broaden your problem-solving skills while learning about new things in the process.

This will force you as well to squash any fear of the unknown. This fear is debilitating and unfounded. It is simply that you do not know what to expect that you have fear about doing certain things. However, nine times out of ten after getting through new situations, you will be better for it, and that fear will no longer exist. The less fear you have, the more you are able to thrive with your psychic skills.

Walk in Other People's Shoes
When you are able to take yourself out of the situation, it will make you a better listener and hone your intuitive skills. This forces you to place yourself in their position

while thinking about what you would do in those same situations given their circumstances.

Practicing this exercise has multi levels of understanding about people. First off, it will help you to see situations from different perspectives while you are learning about their experiences. Another benefit is that you will likely be less judgmental as you will have a deeper knowledge of this person and in turn others.

At the end of the day, you will realize that each person who walks this earth has problems. No one is exempt from this fact and many times there are problems which go on for quite some time be it from complication or ignoring the fact. This may help you also to feel more grateful for the problems that you have, and, perhaps, they are not as bad as you had thought before.

As an added bonus, walking in another's shoes helps you to become more patient. Sometimes talking about issues can be challenging or it may be a complex issue which is complicated to put into words. As this person is possibly mustering up the courage and know how to express their story, you will become patient as you try to understand better what they are going through.

Find your Kindred Spirits

Many times, psychic people may feel isolated from their family members or other people who they come in contact with daily. However, it is very likely that you will have another family member who has the same talents as you. They will be a great guide in asking for the methods that they use to strengthen their own intuitive skills. They can also help you along with issues that you are experiencing as they have most likely gone through the same situation or something similar.

Also, other people who are in a deeper connection with their intuition are able to sense each other. You will likely be drawn to many of them as they will be towards you. When you create a network of people who you can relate to, this not only makes you feel more secure in being an intuitive, but it gives you a support system which is much needed. You will be able to help each other to keep you on the straight and narrow as they will let you know if you seem off or give you techniques to strengthen your skills that had worked for them.

Analyze your Thoughts and Beliefs

Take a long hard look the basis for your beliefs and thoughts as these are going to create the environment within and without you. This includes anything that needs obvious attention such as recurring cycles of unlearned lessons as well as more hidden aspects of yourself. This is the time to be honest with yourself. Only then will you be able to deepen your relationship not only with yourself but with others around you.

When you have predetermined biases and beliefs which have no foundation, this direct affects how you deal with other people. Once these issues are faced head on, you will be able to help others on a more connected nature. It will also aid you in being able to be even more objective about situations.

If you are having issues with finding items which need attention, make a point to dig deeper. We all have biases whether they are based in gender, race or age. We are all unique creatures with special characteristics that we bring to the table. Take this opportunity to learn and to grow, and it will strengthen your empathy even further.

Take this opportunity to let go of negative thoughts, feelings and beliefs which are no longer serving you. Any sort of negativity is going to impede your attitude and growth. When you are harboring these negative thoughts, you are affecting your environment even down the neurochemical level which affects your organs, overall body, your mental attitude and bleeds into your outer environment.

Keep a Curious Mind

Remember when you were a child and you could not satiate your curiosity about everything? This is the mental attitude you need to continue to possess as you grow into adulthood. There is always something to learn. Once you think you know it all, you need to take a step back. Even for talents that you already possess, there is always something that can be perfected or learned about.

There are also other instances where this will come in handy when dealing with people from different walks of life. Perhaps you are dealing with someone who has an unfaltering view which you think is narrow. Or maybe you assume that your green co-worker certain has no knowledge about life. How are you so sure until you ask and dig deeper?

Everyone grows up in different situations and sees the world with a perspective in which you probably do not share. When you delve into learning about these curiosities within other people, you will also look at yourself in a new light. It will in turn help you to understand people better.

Deepen Your Understanding

The best way to understand people better is to ask better thought out questions. The questions which bring about the most interesting insights are intellectual or even provocative. When we talk about the issues in which most people do not bring up in daily interactions, we will learn more as well as see this person perhaps in a different light.

You can practice this with family members, clients or colleagues. Not only will these conversations strengthen your relationship with them, it will give you a broader insight into people from all walks of life. The key is to never think you are ever done with improving yourself or your intuitive skills.

Become more Aware of the Details

There is no doubt that when an intuitive becomes more in tune with the environment within themselves and around them that they are able to pick up on more cues which will aid in becoming even deeply connected. There are a few ways in which someone can foster this exercise.

Firstly, you can sit in a room by yourself. This can be a place that you frequent or a totally new place. Sit quietly without any distractions and take in all the details of the space. Even if you think you know every aspect of your familiar space, make a point to look for the less obvious things. This will train your eye to keep open to new occurrences or even shifts in energy.

Another way is to come up with a mental picture in your mind which is not complex. It can be as simple as a small colored dot or a shape which is in 2D. When first starting out, try to keep your mind focused on this object for at least fifteen seconds or longer if you are able. This will train your mind to not run through so many thoughts, to slow down and to also become more present in the moment.

As you are able to consistently keep this image in your mind for the fifteen second increment, start to add form to your shape, creating a 3D object. To further escalate the exercise, start to rotate the object in your mind's eye and add more detail. Once this accomplished, set your time limit to half a minute.

The point of this exercise is to train your eyes to extract more information from your world around you. After dedicated practice, you will be able to gather details extremely quickly which will assist you in reading people and environments. It may also help you in situations where you are going to need to think very fast.

Focus on your Emotions

You can practice this same idea while focusing on a certain emotion within your heart. This exercise will not even improve your intuitive abilities; it will continue to keep positive emotion in your heart throughout the day while building your institution.

With this technique, you need to feel a deep positive emotion such as affection, joy, kindness, appreciation or love. This emotion is going to consume you first through your whole heart and then vibrate through your mind and body. It will be more powerful if you associate a bright light with this emotion so that you can both visualize and feel this emotion reverberate throughout your body.

Just like the focus exercise, you want to hold this feeling for as long as possible without getting distracted. Put all your energy and focus into this exercise so that it is more impactful. Not only will it strengthen your energy from the inside out, it will develop your visualization skills.

This is also a skill that you will need to develop if you come in contact with energy vampires, narcissists or overall negative people. When this exercise is done around these people, they will likely be aware on the outside. However, you are putting up a barrier so that they are not able to siphon your energy from you.

Deepen Your Objectiveness

When you are objective, you are free of bias and look at all the details in front of you to make a decision or to counsel someone. When you are able to listen from multiple points of view, objectiveness will come to you naturally. To strengthen this skill, you will need to be in contact with people who have different views from your own. Even if they do not think the same way that you do, it does not necessarily mean that they are taking a negative stance. Even knowing the negative side will help you to understand the full spectrum of the situation.

If you have a strong belief about a certain issue such as motorcycle safety for instance, you need to speak to motorcyclists who do not believe in wearing helmets or full protective gear. They may have a different experience than you have which will help you to see the entire picture. This will also break down your judgments of people and help you understand and perceive emotions from different types of people other than who you may be comfortable with.

Listen to Inner Guidance

The best way to strengthen your intuition is to go to the source. Your intuition is that inner voice which is in all people. The sensitive empaths have a fast track to communicating with this inner voice. It is your intuition which has all the answers that you need about your personal growth and healing. This inner voice is always going to lead you to your highest good. It will never make you feel negative feelings and only has love and compassion for you.

The only way to tap into this higher level of intuition is to quiet your mind and clear out what you think you already know. This inner voice can only be heard clearly when all of this clutter is out of the way. This can be done through several methods to include:

Simply being silent in a space which is also quiet Meditation

Prayer or Mantras

Connecting with Nature

When you practice one of the methods at least five minutes a day, you will start to tap into your institution more deeply. This may appear as an epiphany, memory, sound, image, hunch or gut feeling. Those who continue to practice may actually hear their inner voice. When any of these signs make themselves known, you need to acknowledge them. It may also be wise to jot them down in a notebook so that you can expand on this knowledge that you gain at a later time.

Pay Attention to Your Dreams

Dreams are a source of intuition, and they need to have attention paid to them. During REM sleep which occurs approximately every ninety minutes each time you sleep, this is the time that dreams are experienced. These dreams can be excellent guides to show us direction in career choices, relationship, and health among others. The trick is remembering them.

The best way to do this is to keep a dream notebook by your bed. The best time to write is the moment that you wake up because you will remember the most at this time. You may even remember more of the dream as you are writing. When you make a habit of writing down your dreams, this process will become a habit, and it will become much easier to recall the dreams.

If you need some insight on a particular issue, ask a question before going to sleep. Like usual, write down any dreams that you remember, even if it does not seem to answer your question. Each night, ask the same question until you get a more solid answer to your inquiry.

Write It Down

Many times it gets very confusing in an empath's mind, especially when there are many other people's emotions and feelings wrapped up in their own. When you utilize writing down these thoughts that run through your mind, you are able to start deciphering what you are actually feeling compared to the other emotions that you are experiencing.

Not only will this help to raise your awareness, it will also help you to realize when you are soaking up people's energies when you do not intend to. The moment that you start to feel something different than what is true to you personally, you can stop the flow of energy or excuse yourself from this person's presence if possible.

Psychic Skill Development

When you have strengthened your intuition, you will be able to efficiently practice your psychic skill development.

There are many different types of psychic abilities of which I will go over a few in detail. It is possible to have one or a combination of these skills, and to have different intensities of each skill that you can further develop if you wish.

The Basics of Telekinesis

The ability of telekinesis, also known as Psychokinesis, has a certain mysitcal air as you will see this abilitiy in frequently in a sci-fi or horror movie. This is the ability to move or manipulate objects solely with your mind. Psychokinesis is translated from Greek words for motion and mind.

When you view everything in this world and the other planes based in a vibration of energy, you will be more effective in honing your psychic abilities. Items that we see as solid matter are more dense energies where as pure energies that you see and feel are lighter energies with a higher vibration point. When you are using this perspective to work on your telekinesis skills, you will be able to perceive this energy on a personal level and, through practice, be able to manipulate it with the power of your mind.

A summary of the different components of telekinesis is as follows:

❖ Relaxation is required so that you are able to disconnect your body and mind from the every day things that you usually process. When you are able to accomplish this task, you will be in a state of consciousness that you are able to focus and expand upon your thought processes.

❖ Concentration is also a required element as it is ultimately your

will that will help you to be successful at manipulating these energies.

❖ Meditation is a process which will help your mind to accomplish

both relaxation and concentration as you practice any exercise to hone your psychic abilities.

❖ Gratitude is the final component which will help you to strengthen

your connection to the energies outside of yourself. When you are able to demonstrate any of your psychic skills, it is due to the universe for giving you these capabilities, and respect needs to be paid to these energies.

While you are practicing the telekinesis exercises, or any of the psychic skill exercises, you need to have a firm belief that these are very real abilities. When this is in place, no matter the outcome of your exercises, you know that the result was meant to be at that time. You are not always going to be successful, and that is perfectly okay. You are only trying to get back into connection with who you are internally, and there is no wrong way of following this path.

As you continue to practice your psychic exercises and gain some control over them, there will be naysayers who are going to make it their mission that you are crazy for following this dream and that they do not exist. Acknowledge what they are saying, but fall back on your ultimate belief in what you are pursuing.

Recognize that we are all at different levels of development in this soul journey. There is no point in arguing over matters of opinion with a person who is not a master at these skills. Remember, society has molded us into holding these beliefs. If you believe differently, you have this right. At the end of the day, you need to live your life how you see fit, and many people before you have done these same practices with the same goal in mind. Keep an open mind during the exercises, and prepare yourself to be amazed.

Logically thinking about this skill is going to bring about visions of you sitting in your favorite and comfortable chair as you use the power of your mind to bring you everything that you wish. However, telekinesis does not work in this way. When you have mastered the art of telekinesis, you will be able to manipulate small objects.

You must think in terms of energy. It takes an extreme amount of concentration, dedication and practice to be able to strengthen this skill, just to make small amounts of changes. Because of this fact, you are not able to move larger items such as a car or an elephant because of the sheer amount of will power and energy that it requires.

Because of this fact, scientific studies have focused on small and mundane feats such as testing the ability versus probability of a pair of dice landing on a certain number or having an effect on a computerized random number generator. The tests also rely more on complicated analyses of statistics. That is to say, scientists are less interested if a person is able to knock a glass over or bend a spoon. Rather, they would rather test if a person is able to control a coin coming up on tails at a significantly higher percentage than 50%.

Exercises to Develop your Telekinesis
Even with scientific studies resulting in mixed conclusions, there are many people who work at perfecting this skill. While you are practicing these exercises, you must have no doubt in your mind, even on a subconscious level, that you are going to be able to perform telekinesis. You will need to couple your meditations with visualizing exercises.

When you have gotten to the point where you have your mind cleared, select a small and simple object in your surrounding environment and study it so that you are aware of its every detail. Pay special attention to the scent, how soft or hard the object is, color and shape.

After some time of perfecting your visualization skills, close your eyes and visualize your object with every detail you studied. Create a connection by focusing all of your attention to your visualization of this object. Start to make the object move in your visualization how you would like to have the object moved in the physical plane.

Then you will transfer this same energy and intention towards the object in the physical plane. This is best performed by looking at the space between you and the object, then you want to take this space away. Envision you and this object as one with no separation in between.

For the objects that you want to move, it is best to start with something simple such as a matchstick or a pencil. When you are able to successfully move these items, move up to more complicated items such as a glass or lighter.

Continue to practice daily until you start to see results while refining your abilities each time. Over time, hone your visualization skills by expanding the objects that you are envisioning. Step up the objects by complexity and details. After some time of practicing, you can visualize an entire room. The focus of your visualization practices should be getting the visions as detailed as possible.

A specialized meditation practice that you can use is to sit in a comfortable position. After taking a few regular breaths, breathe in deeply for a count of

4. Hold your breath for another count of 4. Then exhale through your mouth for 8 seconds.

After a series of 3 rounds of breath have been completed, let each thought that comes across transform into a sparkle in your field of visualization as you are breathing inwards and while you are holding your breath. As you exhale, allow those sparkles to become one as bright as the sun. Repeat this process as much as necessary until you are finished with your designated meditation time. This exercise will help with both your focus and your visualization skills.

You can also work with your skills by manipulating a candle flame. Light a candle and perform your meditation exercise. Gaze at the flame and let it take over your thoughts. Watch intently and take note when the flame flickers and moves. After your mind is solely concentrated on the flame, try to manipulate which way the flame is going to move with your focused energy.

First move the flame to the left and then to the right. Then try to make the flame grow larger, then make the flame brighter and finally work on having the flame diminish.

With the practice of any of these exercises, you need to stop when you are physically or mental drained. Taking regular breaks if you are extensively practicing is important. Take at least a few hours break if you become tired during these exercises. Make sure that you drink enough water and eat a small snack to keep your energy levels risen. Even if you need a longer break, do not go back to practicing until you are feeling revived in mind and body.

The Basics of Pyrokinesis

Fire is an element which has an underlying fearsome factor, but it is also well known to garnish an impactful amount of power. It was because of fire that the cavemen were able to rise in the food chain above the animals. Likewise, fire can cause a great deal of destruction and hurt. Being able to control the element of fire is the main concept of pyrokinesis.

Pyrokinesis is derived from the Greek word pyro, or fire, and kinesis which is movement. A person who hones this skill is able to manipulate as well as create fires simply by the power of their mind. They do not use any substances to be able to create these flames. Pyrokinesis is a subset of telekinesis because people who are adept at these two practices are able to manipulate the world around them.

As an example of the skill, you can light a stack of paperwork on the floor in the living room. A master at pyrokinesis is able to light this fire with their mind. They will also be able to control that fire so that it will only continue to burn the paper and nothing else or they can dictate the direction in which the fire is going to burn and cause the whole house to burn down if they wish.

There have been no scientific tests to prove the validity of pyrokinesis, but this practice has been practiced with a handful of martial arts practitioners. These masters are able to transform their chi energy so that the heat can be felt in the areas that they choose.

Episodes of spontaneous combustion have also been recorded as far back as 1763. This is where the body of a person catches on fire without any fuel to ignite the fire. This can result in the body smoking and well as the formation of blisters and burns. Others will catch on fire completely, and is seen surprisingly in older people more often. For the firefighters who are familiar with victims of fires, they know that the injuries sustained the typical markers of a fire victim is that their trunk is usually whole while the head and limbs are incarcerated.

However, for the spontaneous combustion cases, it is the opposite with the trunk of the body being nearly gone while the feet and hands remain. It is also a curious case because the flammable items around the body will be in tact with no signs of burning. This makes those who are familiar with spontaneous combustion cases that these fires started from within the truck of their body.

Even though spontaneous combustion is not directly linked to pyrokinesis, there are some striking conclusions which have been logically discussed. One is that these people could be the victims of a person practicing pyrokinetics. Other people believe that it is possible these people were practicing exercises of pyrokinesis and were not able to control the fire completely. It is thought that with this inability to control the fire that they turned it upon themselves which resulted in them spontaneously combusting themselves.

Exercises to Develop your Pyrokinesis

When you train, you will be able to control fire. After a long time of practice, you will be able to extinguish and reignite a flame. You will only be able to hone this skill with continuous practice, unwavering concentration and meditation. Because pyrokinesis can be quite dangerous for beginners, you must be extremely careful when practicing as you will have no control of the fire at first. This is the reason why in many cases training for pyrokinesis should only be done after mastering telekinesis skills.

1.   Light a candle is a space which there are no movements of the air.

2.   Gaze at the flame and concentrate your focus solely on the fire.

3.   Create a connection in your mind between you and the flame.

4.   Close your eyes and envision the flame as vivid and detailed as possible. Feel the energy of the flame within yourself.

5.   Open your eyes and gaze at the flame once more.

6.   Visualize in your mind the flame moving to the right. Do not be upset if this does not occur after many days or months of practicing this feat.

7.   Do not strain yourself and your energy to move the flame. You need to flow with the energy of the flame.

8.　　　　Once you have successfully moved the flame to the right, manipulate it by making it move to the left and also getting larger.

9.　　　　When you are able to manipulate the flame with your willpower, start to practice extinguishing the flame. Take a break if you are straining and stressing your energy.

10.　　　　With this same concentration, envision that the flame is extinguished. This will likely take more time than you mastering manipulating the direction of the flame, so do not get discouraged.

11.　　　　Once you are able to extinguish the fire with your mind, try to reignite the flame. It is simpler if you are able to complete this quickly after the flame has been extinguished.

Another practice you can work with is known as the Dancing Flame.

1.　　Light a candle in a room with no air movement.

2.　　　　Gaze upon the flame as you visualize a tunnel between the flame and you.

3.　　Create a connection of the energy of the flame.

4.　　Once the energy is connected, imagine a sphere of white energy and send it towards the flame through the tunnel.

5.   Now move the sphere in different directions around the candle – higher, lower or to the sides – to manipulate the flame.

6.   After you are able to accomplish this manipulation of the flame, you can move forward to extinguishing the flame.

7.   Place the white energy ball over the flame to remove the oxygen so that the flame will go out.

8.   Remember to take breaks if you are stressing or straining your mind.

The Basics of Empathy

There are several steps that you can take to embrace and strengthen your personal empathic skills. Here there is going to be a comprehensive set of methods to learn more about different empathic skills, way to utilize them for the greatest benefit as well as ways to continue to build up these particular talents.

Every person has the capability of deepening their intuition and empathy levels where you are able to use these God given talents to help not only you, but more importantly the world as a whole. To do this, you must put on your battle face as you are going to be strengthening these attributes by having a strong spirit.

Self-care is the number one step in making sure that you are able to not only use these talents that you have been given, but to continue to work and grow with them. It is a hard process at times, but when has anything not worth having been handed to you on a platter? These methods will take hard work and dedication. You must keep your end goals in mind which will keep your spirit strong during the tough parts of the process so that you can enjoy the full benefits and be able to help others to the best of your ability.

Your self-care is something that comes before any one person or situation. How are you able to help others fully when you are only half energized and centered? These self-care practices will keep your being strong, centered and continue to thrive. When you implement self-care daily, you will become unstoppable as your energy will be reserved for times that you are needing it. It will not continue to be siphoned away by others who are wanting to feed off your energy. You will not take on emotions and feelings that you are not willing to take on. It makes you ever strong in the sensitive world of the empath.

The following are five methods which can be used on a daily basis to continue to build up your strong spirit so that you can then work on strengthening your other empathic skills:

Be Grateful and Express Gratefulness Whenever Possible

When you wake up, start your day on the correct foot by expressing gratitude. First off, there are many people who did not get the same privilege. At the very least, you should be grateful about you breathing, your health, and other blessings including family and being able to help others.

You can continue to find gratefulness in the difficult situations that you possess. These are the greatest things to be grateful for because they are in your life to teach you the most. When you can change your perspective on these "bad" things, it will lift you up even higher in your gratitude.

When you practice gratitude on a daily basis as part of your self-care, it makes you more self-aware, keeps you in the moment and builds positive energy. It also will keep you more energized as you will not be bleeding energy by imagining things that will happen in the future or wasting worry on things that have happened in the past.

You can also utilize this method throughout the day to continue building up the positive energy. Take the time to express your gratitude to the people who you come in contact with, your pets and your family members. You can extend this idea even to strangers who you can change their attitude with a simple smile. This also shows them appreciation in a subtle way. All of these little gestures add up and will continue to strengthen you throughout the day.

Love Yourself Fully

Recognize daily that you are unique individual that has a purpose in this world. You are a gift, and you are here to share and meld with the other gifts in this world. Consider coming up with a phrase or mantra which is special to you that will help you lift yourself up. If you are coming up with your own, try to incorporate all aspects of you in a short sentence which is powerful and impactful to your spirit and well-being.

Other ways that you can love yourself is to listen to your body and adjust your day accordingly. Do not try to push yourself to the point where you are breaking when you are just waking up in the morning. Just like you need to stretch to warm up your body before exercise, you must allow yourself to wake up properly so that you are centered and focused on the tasks of the day.

Whatever makes you the happiest in your soul whether it is reading a certain book of inspiring quotes or drinking your favorite tea while watching the birds play out in your yard, take the time to nurture your spirit in the morning times, especially, even though this also can be applied throughout the day.

The properly love yourself, you must be quiet and listen to yourself so that you will know what your needs are. Once these needs are met, you will be able to be your full self to be able to share your healing energy with other people in a more impactful and helpful way.

Aware and Mindful Breathing

At some point during your morning routine, likely coupled with the meditation exercise, you need to empty your energy and spirit of any negativity and stress. This will not only help to calm your inner self; it will give you a sense of clarity and strengthen your energy throughout the day.

You are going to want to try to do this at the same time of the day and you can do this exercise at any time that you are feeling stress build up in your body. This will help you to keep your focus throughout the day as well. The morning exercise should be a minimum of ten minutes, but you can do whatever time length you feel comfortable as long as your stress and negativity is melted away.

The mindful breathing exercise is as follows:

1.   Find a place in which you feel comfortable and shake the extremities of your body before you sit or lay down to help with the process of relaxation.

2.   Breathe in deeply and long in through your nose while allowing your stomach to fill with air.

3.   Hold the air for a few seconds.

4.   Slowly let the air out through your mouth.

5.   Do this practice for a minimum of three breaths before moving onto the next part of the exercise.

For the next section, you need to visualize a situation, place or phrase which brings you to a place of relaxation. Once you find this calm, continue on.

1.   Close your eyes and continue to breath in through your nose.

2.   As you are breathing, visualize the air you are breathing is full of calm and peace. Allow this feeling to immolate throughout your body.

3.   Then breathe out slowly through your mouth while visualizing any tension or stress in your body leaving with the breath.

4.　　　　Continue to breathe in and out using the visualizations for the remainder of your breathing exercise time, for a minimum of ten minutes.

5.　　　Continue on to the meditation practice if you wish for your daily self-care.

Exercises to Develop your Empathy

The Basics of Astral Projection

This is a skill that can be perfected which will allow you to have an out of body experience or a state of consciousness which is altered. It is experienced when your spirit is able to physically leave your body so that you can travel through different dimensions. Your spirit is not entirely detached from your body as there is a silver cord similar to an umbilical cord which keep the two connected. This cord is not able to be detached except through death, so there is no possibility of this cord breaking while your spirit is out of your body.

There is not simply one experience that you have when you astral project. Some people says that you can experience sensations of floating or flying in the sky while you are able to look down upon the world. You can also experience the world as if you were standing in the room, yet no one would be able to see and interact with you. Lucid dreaming is a type of astral projection since you are conscious of your activities during the sleep state.

Exercises to Develop your Astral Travel Skills

Like all of the other physic abilities, you need to use meditation to keep your mind focused and quiet. You will need to remove any doubts that you are able to accomplish and hone this skill, as these doubts will surely keep you from experiencing an out of body experience. You need to ensure that the space that you choose to astral project from is a comfortable temperature. It is also important to make sure that you are not going to get hungry, but do not eat a large meal ahead of time, otherwise you will likely go to sleep.

1.   Sit or lay in a spot where you will not be disturbed. All the muscles in your body to relax.

2.   Take deep and slow breaths in through your nose and out through your mouth.

3.   Concentrate your focus on creating a white light which will cover your entire body.

4.   Once you envision your body is covered in white light, imagine that it is floating up slowly.

5.   As you see your body rising, your spirit and body will separate in your mind, leaving the physical body

where you first started. The spirit body is going to rise above the physical body.

6.   Remove any fear or doubt in your mind. Choose a destination you would like to experience.

7.   Once you have projected to another location and you want to return back, simply think of your physical body, and envision your spirit entering your physical body slowly.

Another method that you can use is known as The Rope

1.   Envision yourself laying down with a rope laying on top of you.

2.   Then imagine that you reach your hands out to the rope and start pulling yourself upwards.

3.   Continue to pull upwards on the rope until you start to feel a vibration throughout your entire body.

4.   As you continue to pull on the rope, you will start to feel the sensation of flying. This is when your spirit has separated from your physical body.

5.   Let the rope go, and look downwards to see yourself lying down.

6.   Return to your body by thinking of your spiritual body slowly entering your physical body once again.

One last technique was created by Muldoon, and it is known as his Thirst Technique. For this exercise, you need to refrain from drinking water throughout the entire day you want to practice. You will be using your want and need for water as an emotion which will drive you to bartering for an out of body experience.

1.   Pour yourself a glass of water in a clear cup. Place it on a table in front of you.

2.   Gaze at the glass of water as you imagine yourself drinking the water. Continue this practice for three hours.

3.   Before you go to sleep, set the glass of water within a few feet of you and eat a pinch of salt. This will cause you to be craving water more.

4.   As you lie in bed, continue to imagine yourself getting up out of bed and drinking the glass of water.

5.   You will know this exercise is successful if you are able to astral project and drink the water in your spirit form.

The Risks and Benefits of Psychic Skills
There are some perks to being tapped and connected with your psychic skills. Once you start to delve deeper within this connection, you will realize that these benefits will touch on all areas of your life and bond you closer to yourself, your environment and those close to you.

It is important to note that these skills also come with their own responsibilities because if you use them for your personal benefit of an ill intention, they can quickly start to cause havoc in your life as well as others. An example of this would be someone who is able to see future events. Remember that the future is not static and is based upon possibilities. Refrain from telling people that something is sure to happen because their personal choices may change the outcome of your vision for their future.

You will start to see the world from a unique and different perspective. You will also have more clear insight into how to make decisions which will be for your greatest benefit and choosing the correct path for you. You will also feel more tapped in and find there is a natural flow of energy that takes you through life. You will be able to feel more at peace knowing that you have nothing truly to worry about because it is all part of a larger plan.

When you tap into these psychic energies, you need to be aware that they can come at a cost. They are meant to connect you to something much greater outside of yourself, but it must be respected. If you are wanting to strengthen these skills just to get personal gain, you are likely going to see a ripple effect of terrible things infiltrating your life and those surrounding you. Let me go over the main difficulties that you may face when you are learning about your skills and if you should use them for the wrong purpose.

There is a limit to the storage space of the energy within your system. While you are cultivating your skills, these energy levels will rise. Your body is able to adapt to these fluctuations in energy, and your space is going to grow over time. However, if you try to take on too many energies before your body adapts, it will result in overload of your system. You will simply will not be able to handle above and beyond the space that you body has dedicated to handling these energies.

The symptoms when you take on too much energy will be dizziness and headaches. You may feel like you have ADHD because you will lack the ability to focus, resulting in you lose your psychic skills temporarily. You may feel lost as you are swimming through the heightened amount of energy flowing through your body. If this should occur, consciously bring yourself down by grounding and centering yourself so that your energy will naturally neutralize. Take some time to nurture yourself by taking some alone time to revitalize your body.

In this same effect, you may be in the position where you are taking on too much information as you are developing your psychic skills. As you delve deeper into the process, you may come across information which may be an epiphany which your mind is not able to fully handle or comprehend at the moment. It may completely negative a firmly held belief you have had your entire life.

This is usually the case if you are working to build your psychic skills each day as a beginner. Be sure to listen to your body and your mind as you are going through this process. Do not push yourself if you should be feeling tired or hungry. If you are feeling particularly stressed, take care of your physical self before you venture into your spiritual side.

If you are gifted with the vision of spirits, this may be an interesting and wanted experience, when it happens occasionally. However, the more that some people deepen their connection to the other side, they are able to see spirits all of the time as they mingle with living people. It may get to the point where you are not able to determine if they are spirits or living people, which can pose a problem.

If this should happen, be sure to talk to your other psychic friends to get support. They may also have some very good advice as to how to handle this. Grounding yourself on a daily basis will help this from occurring. Meditation is also very helpful to help continue to calm and focus your mind.

As you strengthen your intuitive and empathic skills, you may find that you are able to experience other people's pain and emotions. This can drive a person a bit mad if they are unaware that this wide range of symptoms and emotions that they are feeling are not actually their own. When you have other people's emotions mixed with your own, they can be conflicting, which makes you feel confused within yourself.

If you find that you are empathic in this way, make sure that you learn how to shield your energy from other people so that they are not able to meld with your own. Essentially you are building a protective bubble which cannot be penetrated. This will also help you in the case that other people are trying to drain you of your own energy.

Chapter 14 Root Chakra Reiki Meditation for Day One Through Three

Overview of the Mooladhara Chakra Root or 1st Chakra

Associated with the earth element, the purpose of this chakra is to give a firm foundation, support, stability and safety. It is associated with the sciatic nerve, bones, legs, feet. It is the location of the energy of existence. It connects our energy to the material world as well as primal survival. The color which is connected with the root chakra is red.

When this chakra is clear and balanced, you will feel happy to be alive as well as worthy of your existence. However, when this chakra is in need of work because of it being blocked, our perspective changes. We feel entitled to occupy our space or we may feel a lack of love or value. This negative thinking leads us to resent our existence as well as compare ourselves with others.

As you work on balancing the mooladhara chakra, you will start to trust in the flow of prosperity in all forms in your life. You will also strengthen your overall wellbeing and health along with your sense of security. Exercises based on opening and charging the 1st chakra contains the pranic energy. It also is the place in which our hidden or darker sides of our nature are concealed, sometimes even from ourselves.

Responsibilities of the Root Chakra

It is extremely important to pay special attention to the 1st chakra because making sure that it is healed, cleared, opened and balanced is key for the other chakras to do the same. This is the energy center where all of your basic needs are addressed. The term Muladhara translates into base or root support. The main influences of the root chakra are the following:

❖ You confidence levels

❖ Your survival

❖ Your sense of security and safety

❖ Your drive for basic physical needs like rest, shelter and food

❖ Your feeling of being grounded

Imbalance Symptoms

A root chakra imbalance can easily throw your entire system out of order. When your base chakra is in alignment, you will feel an overall peace while also feeling comfortable with your life, relaxed and stable. However, when this chakra is misaligned or blocked, you will feel quite insecure as well as worried about your basic needs. It will also raise your anxiety and stress levels as you continue to worry. You may also have problems with one or a combination of the following:

❖   Feeling overwhelmed easily by bright lights, loud noises or crowds

Major illness plague you such as depression,fibromyalgia, fatigue and chronic pain

❖   Overly care for people who are physically and mentally able.

❖   Heightened feeling of panic or being threatened which can lead to racing heart, hyperventilation and panic attacks.

❖   Overall feeling of uncertainty

❖   Lack of concentration due to preoccupation with worry.

- ❖ Cold extremities

- ❖ Low energy levels

- ❖ Sore lower back

- ❖ Pain in the legs

- ❖ Digestive upset

- ❖ Negativity towards yourself and other people

- ❖ An unhealthy relationship with food such as purging, binging or starving.

- ❖ Low self-confidence levels

- ❖ Extreme reliance on external feedback for validation

These imbalances and blockages can happen due to a singular event such as a conflict with a friend of family member, financial difficulties or losing a job suddenly.

Day 1 Root Chakra Physical Meditation

It is important to have your chakras straightened and centered before performing grounding and meditation practices. This ensures that your energy is flowing properly throughout your body and will bring the best benefit to your grounding and meditation exercises.

Be sure to perform this each day before you start your meditation practice.

To center yourself, you will simply:

1. Stand up straight with your hands down by your side. You can stand against a wall to ensure your body is straight.

Alternatively, you can do this exercise while sitting down with your feet flat on the floor.

2. Visualize a line going from the top of your head down through your back straight down to the ground.

You can now move onto the practice of grounding. It is a simple practice that can be done practically anywhere. It is best to do this outside where you are able to place your bare feet on the ground. However, the same principle can occur anywhere, even with shoes on. The point of this exercise is to make you feel more connected with the earth as well as being fully present in the moment within your body.

To ground yourself:

1. Stand outside on the dirt, grass or sit in a chair with your feet firmly planted on the ground.

2.   Breathe deep through your mouth. As you are breathing in, visualize white light encompassing your body.

3.   As you breathe out through your nose, direct the breath visually down   through your feet.

4.   Continue with this cycle of breathing until the sense of calmness overtakes you again which usually takes a minimum of three breaths.

The follow through to the physical root chakra meditation:

1.   While starting this mediation, breathe with intent while focusing your attention to the base of your spine, the location of the root chakra.

2.   While standing in a comfortable position, make fists out of your hands and hold them tight for two to three seconds.

3.   Continue to clench your fists for five rounds.

4.   Shake your hands to release the energy and allow them to become relaxed.

5.   Then rub your hands together for several seconds until you feel them become warm and electrified.

6.   Clap your hands together forcefully once the point has been reached that your hands are full of electric pulses.

7.   Put one foot out in front of you while pointing your toes. Hold for a couple of seconds.

8.   Move your foot up and down vertically to stretch out your ankles while holding in both positions for a couple of seconds.

9.   Repeat the last two steps with your other foot.

10.   Set your hands on your knees and quickly rub your thighs up towards your hips and then back to your knees.

11.   Repeat this step a few times or until heat is generated in your thighs.

12.   Now stand straight with your hands resting by your side.

13.   Raise one hand above your head as high as you can as you breath in through   your nose.

14.   Then lower your hand slowly as you breath out through your mouth.

15.   Repeat with your other hand and practice this for a few rounds.

16.   Once complete, leave your arms loosely at your sides as you rest for a moment.

17.   During this rest period, intently pay attention to your energy levels in the root chakra as you mindfully breathe in and out.

18.   Continue to release any negativity and stress in your 1st

chakra with each breath out. Breathe in healing and positive energy.

19.   Now take a walk in the park or in nature for a period that you set so that you can recharge and balance your first chakra.

Day 2 Root Chakra Mental Meditation

1.   Sit on the floor in a cross legged or kneeling position. Alternatively, you can sit in a chair with your feet flat on the floor.

2.   Keep your shoulders, back and your spine straight.

3.   Relax all your muscles, closing your eyes and take a few normal breaths.

4.   Inhale deeply and fully through the nose. Pull the breath as far down into your body as you can. Exhale slowly through the mouth.

Repeat for 3 breaths.

5.   Then turn your focus to the area of the root chakra. Take note of any tightness in the area.

6.   Envision a ball of red energy at your root chakra. Manipulate this ball in your mind so that it expands. Then start to see it spin.

7.   As the red ball of energy grows, feel the sensation of your root chakra as it becomes relaxed and warm.

8.   Once your 1st chakra feels warm, continue to meditate while feeling this sensation of warmth between five and ten minutes.

9.   With every breathe in, see and believe that you are breathing in positive and healing energy. While you breathe out, envision you release the negative, stagnant and stale energy.

10.   When you have completed, slowly open your eyes.

11.   Rest in this space for a few minutes before trying to get up.

Day 3 Root Chakra Spiritual Meditation

Each chakra has what is known as a beej mantra which is a word from Sanskrit. Chanting these mantras create a specific sound and vibration which resonates with each chakra in a unique way, helping to clear and balance your energy centers as well as connecting you to the higher power outside of yourself.

1. Sit comfortably in a meditation posture which is comfortable for you. This can be on a yoga mat, cushion or a chair.

2. Close your eyes and take in three normal breaths, focusing on the flow of the air throughout your body.

3. Concentrate upon your root chakra as you envision red throughout your sight of vision.

4. Take note how the color makes you feel.

5. Place the tip of your tongue on the back section of the upper palate on the roof of your mouth.

6. Focus the red into a sphere at the base of your spine.

7. As you breathe in, focus your concentration on the sphere.

8. Chant the sound "loom" for each slow release of breath as you envision the red sphere vibrating.

9. With each breathe, see the sphere getting larger and more vibrant.

10. Continue chanting between three and five minutes as you continue to concentrate on the root chakra sensations.

11. As you breathe in, fill yourself with positive energies. Allow the breath as it exits your body to take away any of the blockages and tension that you feel.

12. When the exercise is complete, slowly open your eyes and take your time moving when you are comfortable to do so.

Chapter 15 Sacral Chakra Reiki Meditation Day Four Through Six

Overview of the Svadhisthana Chakra - Sacral or 2nd Chakra

The sacral chakra is associated with the element of water. The purpose is to allow pleasure, emotional wellbeing, expansion, flow and movement. The areas of the body which are connected with this chakra are the joints, inner thighs, sex organs, lower abdomen,

sacrum and hips. The color of orange is associated with the sacral chakra. It is also responsible for helping us to trust our sensation. As we are drawn to the things that make us feel good, this chakra is starting to open up. When we trust our instincts, we are able to surrender to our highest consciousness and allow nature to work her creative force through us.

When this chakra is blocked, which means the pranic energy is not able to freely flow, we no longer have the trust as we have lost the connection to our intuition and source of our feelings. As we are separated from our higher power, we start to feel negativity, lethargy and depression. If you are a person who must be in control of their lives, it is usually because the 2nd chakra is out of balance as you feel as if everything is out of control. The truth is, you must accept that much of everything is out of your control.

Only when this thought of control is surrendered will you feel more at peace.

Responsibilities of the Sacral Chakra

The 2nd chakra is related to anything to do with creation and creativity. It also has an association to personal growth, imagination and sex drive. It is located in the middle of the abdomen about two inches below the belly button. It influences your feeling of:

❖ Feedback of artistic pursuits

❖ Your confidence level in what you create

❖ Pleasure you feel in life

❖ Satisfaction in romantic relationship

❖ Ability to be playful with others

❖ Inspiration level you experience

Imbalance Symptoms

When this chakra is open, you have an overall feeling of being stimulated as well-being full of ideas. You will also feel heightened confidence to proceed with significant changes in your lifestyle. However, when this chakra is out of balance, your life will feel stifling, repetitive and boring. Your sacral chakra can become quickly closed if you have any negative feedback about sexuality or creativity. Other common symptoms are:

❖ Losing sleep while worrying too much or heightened anxiety level

❖ Suffer from passive aggressiveness and resentfulness when others only take from them

❖ Isolating themselves from other people and normal activities

❖ Becoming addicted to substances such as alcohol, medications or illegal drugs

❖ Lack of creativity

❖ Cyclical dysfunctional relationships

❖ Lack of motivation

❖ Diminished sexual appetite or unpleasant sexual intercourse

- ❖ Emotional confusion

- ❖ You feel unimportant and thinks that no one loves you

- ❖ You cannot take care of yourself or you feel you do not know how

- ❖ You tend to hang your shoulders bent forward

- ❖ Easily offended

- ❖ Fear of change

- ❖ Massive amounts of guilt about the past

- ❖ Low self-worth

- ❖ Frequent bouts of jealousy

- ❖ Heightened issues with allergy symptoms

- ❖ Bladder discomfort

- ❖ Low energy

- ❖ Gambling, shopping addiction and eating issues

Some common causes of these symptoms are based on associations with sexuality, creativity and change. You may find that you have sexual incompatibility in a relationship, rejection of your creative words, reproductive issues or rejection from a crush or love.

This chakra is associated with water which means that any activities in body of water will help balance the energy. If you are not around any sources of water, a long and soothing bath will do the trick as well. When you eat foods which are orange such as mangoes, melons, oranges or carrots, you will clear this chakra.

Day 4 Sacral Chakra Physical Meditation

To enhance this meditation, you can perform it by a body of water such as a lake, river or ocean. If these are not available and you would like to incorporate this idea into your meditation, you can also draw a bath.

1.   Sit comfortably in a meditation posture which is comfortable for you. This can be on a yoga mat, cushion or a chair.

2.   Close your eyes and take in three normal breaths, inhaling through your nose and breathing out through your mouth.

3.   Envision a stream of light shining down on the top of your head and having the light flow through your body all the way to your toes.

4.   This light is going to wash away any tension that is present in your body as you allow your muscles to loosen and relax.

5.   Now imagine that light slowing moving up your legs up to your waist. Pause it there for a short time, as you feel comfortable.

6.   Then push this light up to your chest and covering your shoulders and back.

7.   Allow this light to flow down your arms to the tips of your fingers.

8.   Push this light up your neck, throat, face up to the top of your head.

9.   Sit while focusing on your breathing as well as the sensations that are felt throughout your body for a minimum of 10 minutes.

10.   When you are ready, slowly open your eyes and take note of your quality of your mind afterwards. Make an intention to keep your mind in this space throughout the day.

Day 5 Sacral Chakra Mental Meditation

1.   Sit in a comfortable and quiet place. Keep your back and neck straight with your limbs relaxed.

2.   Take ten slow, deep breaths in through your nose and out through your mouth.

3.   Envision a spinning orange sphere at your sacral chakra.

4. Imagine the orange light rippling outwards until it covers your entire body.

5. Feel the sensation that your body is warming up.

6. Continue to focus on your breath and keep feeling this orange energy for a minimum of five minutes.

7. When you are ready, slowly open your eyes and take your time getting back up on your feet.

8. Do this for as long as you like (preferably for at least five minutes), then open your eyes when you're ready.

Day 6 Sacral Chakra Spiritual Meditation

1. Sit comfortably in a meditation posture which is comfortable for you. This can be on a yoga mat, cushion or a chair.

2. Close your eyes and take in three normal breaths, focusing on the flow of the air throughout your body.

3. Concentrate upon your sacral chakra as you envision orange throughout your sight of vision.

4. Take note how the color makes you feel as your body starts to warm up.

5. Place your upper set of teeth on the inner section of your lower lip.

6.   In this position, you will sound similar to a car revving up when you breath out.

7.   Focus on the orange sphere, as you breathe in. Focus your concentration on the sphere.

8.   Chant the sound "vahm" for each slow release of breath as you envision the red sphere vibrating.

9.   With each breathe, see the sphere getting larger and more vibrant.

10.   Continue chanting between three and five minutes as you continue to concentrate on the 2nd chakra sensations.

11.   As you breathe in, fill yourself with positive energies. Allow the breath as it exits your body to take away any of the blockages and tension that you feel.

12.   When the exercise is complete, slowly open your eyes and take your time moving when you are comfortable to do so.

Chapter 16 Solar Plexus Chakra Reiki Meditation Day Seven Through

Nine

Overview of the Manipura Chakra - Solar Plexus or 3rd Chakra

This chakra is associated with fire and has the purpose of change, transformation, willpower, strength and energy. The ribs, adrenal glands, digestive organs and upper abdomen are associated with the 3rd chakra. When there are any issues with these parts of the body, this chakra is in need of attention and energetic cleansing. The navel was where everyone was once connected to their mothers through the umbilical cord. Of course, we relied in this cord for our connection and nutrients from our mother. Even after the umbilical cord is cut, this connection will always be present in the navel.

On an energetic level, this chakra holds the power and consciousness of our spiritual selves. As the prana flows through our manipura chakra, is gives the sustained energy the same as the sunshine. This is why the color yellow is associated with this chakra. It also gives us the capability of manifesting with confidence on this plane.

In the case of Kundalini awakening, the 3rd chakra is where the true awakening happens as this is the location where the internal fire is ignited and sent through to the other chakras. It is also the seat of our gut instinct as we feel if something is off in this chakra. These messages are extremely important to listen to as this is the connection to our internal guidance system.

If this chakra is out of balance, you will feel uncertain about your choices as well as your day-to-day decisions. As you work on opening and clearing the navel chakra, you will feel a sense of balance and you will be more sensitive to the messages from your gut instinct. Once you start to practice listening, you will be able to feel as if you are in the correct flow with the universe.

Responsibilities of the Solar Plexus

The 3rd chakra is in direct alignment with your ability to cultivate your skill and make the best decisions because you will be able to see the bigger picture of a situation. You will also experience heightened confidence and self-esteem levels. It is located in the stomach area at the top of your abdomen and is commonly known as the personal power chakra. The solar plexus is responsible for the following:

❖   How you define your purpose

❖   Your level of independence

❖   If you learn lessons from difficult situations

❖   Self-discipline levels

❖   Your ability for self-forgiveness

❖   Whether you envision yourself as being good enough

❖   Your response to criticism from others.

Imbalance Symptoms

With the 3rd chakra in balance, you will be certain of the steps needed to succeed, you are sure of your identity and are self-assured. When this chakra is out of balance, you will find that you will have difficulty with sudden changes or moving from your past mistakes. You are also able to have an oversensitive chakra when out of alignment which may lead to anxiety issues or mania. Symptoms you may experience when the solar plexus is not open are:

❖   Not exercising personal boundaries or standing up for themselves

❖   Attracting energy vampires and negative people

❖ Cannot let things go and soak up toxic and negative energy

❖ Low self-esteem levels

❖ Lack of direction or purpose

❖ Feeling helpless

❖ Feeling the need to control everyone and everything around you

❖ Feelings of worthlessness

❖ Nausea

❖ Bloating

❖ Short-term memory issues

❖ Digestive cramps

The element for this chakra is fire. Create a bonfire and sit around it while basking in the fire. Alternatively, sit in the bright afternoon sunshine for at least twenty minutes. Changes in the diet should include yellow foods such as corn, pineapple, turmeric, ginger and bananas.

The element for this chakra is fire. Create a bonfire and sit around it while basking in the fire. Alternatively, sit in the bright afternoon sunshine for at least twenty minutes. Changes in the diet should include yellow foods such as corn, pineapple, turmeric, ginger and bananas.

Day 7 Solar Plexus Chakra Physical Meditation

1.   Sit in a comfortable position and take note about your mental and physical state.

2.   Take a few deep breaths while inhaling through your nose and exhaling through your mouth.

3.   As you exhale, release the tension and pressure within your body and mind.

4.   If there are any tense areas of your body, focus you attention by relaxing them on each exhale.

5.   Envision a place in your mind where you are completely calm and at ease.

6.   Be detailed about your picture of your happy place with all of the smells, sounds and sights you can experience.

7.   Continue to breathe slowly and deeply as you continue to envision and enjoy this space you have created for a minimum of five minutes.

8.   Create a space where all of your dreams and aspirations are true for you. Take note of how this space makes you feel as you build yourself higher.

9. When you are ready, slowly open your eyes and reflect on your feelings towards yourself.

10. Take your time getting back up on your feet.

Day 8 Solar Plexus Chakra Mental Meditation

1. Sit in a comfortable spot where you will not be disturbed.

2. Take in a few deep and long breaths in through your nose and out through your mouth as you clear your mind.

3. Focus your attention on your solar plexus chakra.

4. Envision a sphere of yellow at the center of your chakra. Take the time to grow the sphere in size and intensity.

5. Manipulate the sphere to spin as it is growing. You will find that your body is going to grow warm during this process.

6. Sit in this space while controlling your breath between three to five minutes.

7. Take notice of how the energy makes your body feel inside and out.

8. When you are ready to open your eyes, take three additional deep breaths before doing so.

Day 9 Solar Plexus Chakra Spiritual Meditation

1.   Sit comfortably in a meditation posture which is comfortable for you. This can be on a yoga mat, cushion or a chair.

2.   Close your eyes and take in three normal breaths, focusing on the flow of the air throughout your body.

3.   Concentrate your attention of the lower middle section of your back. Envision yellow throughout your sight of vision.

4.   Take note how the color makes you feel.

5.   Place the tip of your tongue on the front section of the upper palate near your teeth on the roof of your mouth.

6.   Focus the yellow into a sphere at the spine where you have focused concentration.

7.   As you breathe in, focus your concentration on the sphere.

8.   Chant the sound "rrahm" by rolling the "r"for each slow release of breath as you envision the yellow sphere vibrating.

9.   With each breathe, see the sphere getting larger and more vibrant.

10.   Continue chanting between three and five minutes as you continue to concentrate on the root chakra sensations.

11.   As you breathe in, fill yourself with positive energies. Allow the breath as it exits your body to take away any of the blockages and tension that you feel.

12.   When the exercise is complete, slowly open your eyes and take your time moving when you are comfortable to do so.

Chapter 17 Heart Chakra Reiki Meditation Day Ten Through Twelve

Overview of the Anahata Chakra - Heart or 4th Chakra

The air is associated with the heart chakra. It is commonly known to have the purpose of union, connection, relationships, expansion and love. The parts of the body that are associated with the 4th chakra are the shoulder blades, respiratory system, heart, ribs, diaphragm,

lungs and chest. This is an important chakra to have cleared and energized as it helps you to relate to others outside of yourself.

The color which is connected with this chakra is green and it is the most powerful chakra center in the human body. When Kundalini energy is released from the navel to the heart chakra, it brings a cascade of spiritual, emotional and physiological changes. We are able to resonate with the truth of our feelings when this occurs as the heart has the capability of transcending everything.

When we are doing anything based in emotions, they are based in the heart chakra. It could be a memory, vulnerability or even when we are speaking to others in a heartfelt way. It is through the 4th chakra that we are able to inspire other people. When this chakra has been activated, it is not solely depending on outside sources. In fact, internally you need to experience empathy which is self-sustaining and deep to fully connect with yourself and others.

When the anahata chakra is out of balance, you do not pay attention and ignore your own needs. You may also start to cling to others and become codependent for the support that you require rather than giving that support to yourself. Of course, when you start to clear and charge this chakra, you will become more compassionate and giving to yourself and others.

The heart chakra is positioned directly above the heart. So, slightly to the left at the center of your chest. Sometimes called the Anahata, it both responds to and helps to shape your capacity for compassion, affection, and love.

Responsibilities of the Heart Chakra

The 4th chakra is located in the middle of your chest next to your chest. It is a type of bridge between your spirituality, emotions and thought. You heart chakra has a connection with:

❖ How much peace you feel

❖ Your capacity to self-reflect

❖ Knowledge of self

❖ Emotional openness

❖ Intensity that you are able to care about others

❖ Your level of empathy

Imbalance Symptoms

When your heart chakra is balanced, you are a giving and compassionate person who is also calm and loving. This is directed towards yourself and others, and you keep boundaries well for your own well-being. When it is not open, you are going to feel emotionally hurt for anything that does not happen your way. It can also quickly drain your emotional resources. Other symptoms include:

❖ Putting other people's needs first and showing codependent tendencies

❖ Staying in an abusive or negative relationship

❖ Attract bullies and narcissist personalities lack of empathy

❖ Irritability or impatience

❖ Difficulty in trusting other people

❖ Restlessness

❖ A decrease in the effectiveness of the immune system

❖ Raised or high blood pressure

❖ Insomnia

❖ Struggle to relate to others

Toxic and difficult romantic and non-romantic relationships can quickly close off the heart chakra. You might be dealing with an intense number of emotions that you do not know how to deal with, loss or grief, cutting ties with someone or a lover who does not reciprocate. You can also be having a hard time accepting a specific truth about yourself.

The air is associated with the heart chakra. Deep breathing exercises will eliminate the blocked energy. You could also take a boat ride, fly a kite or open the windows of your home, office or car. Green foods will clear this chakra. Examples include spinach, kale, avocado and broccoli.

Day 10 Heart Chakra Physical Meditation

1.   Sit on a cushion or a chair with your feet flat on the ground. Relax your muscles as you take a few deep and long breaths. Breathe in through your nose and out through your mouth smoothly.

2.   Close your eyes slowly and envision a flame within your heart chakra as you continue with your smooth and long breaths.

3.   Keep the flame burning steady. You will notice that any distractions to your thoughts or otherwise is going to cause the flame to flicker and waver.

4.   Keep this meditation and concentration on keeping the flame constant for a minimum of ten minutes, but no more than half an hour.

5.   When you are ready, slowly open your eyes and continue to breathe steadily until you are ready to stand up.

Day 11 Heart Chakra Mental Meditation
1.   Sit in a comfortable, relaxing place where you will not be disturbed.

2. Breathe in through your nose and out through your mouth for three minutes. Continue to relax your muscles as you breathe.

3. Envision green energy flowing up through your body towards the heart starting at the 1st chakra.

4. Picture the green energy creating a sphere at your heart chakra. As you inhale and exhale, see that ball becoming larger and more vibrant.

5. Focus on tuning into feelings of love for yourself and others as you allow the green energy to permeate your whole body.

6. Continue this meditation between three and five minutes.

7. Carefully open your eyes slowly and take your time getting back to your feet.

Day 12 Heart Chakra Spiritual Meditation

1. Sit comfortably in a meditation posture which is comfortable for you. This can be on a yoga mat, cushion or a chair.

2. Close your eyes and take in three normal breaths, focusing on the flow of the air throughout your body.

3. Concentrate upon your heart chakra as you envision green throughout your sight of vision.

4.   Take note how the color makes you feel.

5.   Focus the green into a sphere on your spine behind your heart chakra.

6.   As you breathe in through your mouth, chant the sound "yum" as the air fills your mouth and throat.

7.   With each breathe, see the sphere getting larger and more vibrant.

8.   Continue chanting for a minimum of 10 minutes up to half an hour as you continue to concentrate on the heart chakra sensations.

9.   As you breathe in, fill yourself with positive energies. Allow the breath as it exits your body to take away any of the blockages and tension that you feel.

10.   When the exercise is complete, slowly open your eyes and take your time moving when you are comfortable to do so.

Chapter 18 Throat Chakra Reiki Meditation Day Thirteen Through Fifteen

Overview of the Vishuddha Chakra - Throat or 5th Chakra

The element of sound is associated with the throat chakra where refinement, purification and communication is the purpose. The body parts which are associated with the 5th chakra are the ears, mouth, tongue, throat, neck and shoulders. If there is any sort of imbalance with these areas of your body, you are in need of clearing and charging of the vishuddha chakra.

Because the 5th chakra corresponds to the throat, it is the energy center in which we are able to speak with our authentic voice. It is where choices turn into actions and allows us to make focused choice on how we want to communicate with others. The color which is used with this chakra is blue. It is where our true self originates as we express who we are with the outside world.

When you realize that this chakra is not receiving pranic energy, you will have expressing emotions or true thoughts. You will put out a kind face to the world and try to be polite at all times when in truth it is not resonating with how you feel in your heart. This is a form of denying your truth which is what causes the blockages in this chakra. When you start to work on opening the throat chakra, you will be able to express your true feelings and thoughts without fear in a loving way.

If everything in your life is going well, all of these chakras will be aligned and in harmony. You'll be happy, healthy and at peace. In contrast, a blockage in one or more of the chakras can make you feel profoundly unsettled.

Responsibilities of the Throat Chakra

The throat chakra is located in the middle of your throat and is connected to your communication and self-expression skills. It will have an impact on:

❖ Awareness of your needs

❖ Your capability to be heard

❖ The quality of your relationships

❖ How you react to confrontation or conflict

❖ If you live your life authentically

❖ Your emotional honesty

Imbalance Symptoms

When this 5th chakra is open, you will be able to communicate clearly and be able to express any of your views with tact. You will have an understanding of what you need and be able to put your words across in ways that people will want to listen. When the throat chakra is out of balance, you will find that you feel that people do not listen to you and you will have difficulty communicating with others.

❖ Unable to stop listening to someone who is venting or spouting off with negativity

Listening to people's problems even when it is inconvenient

❖ Feeling like people do not know the real you

❖ Feel like you have many secrets

❖ Lacking the words to describe your emotions

❖ An achy or stiff neck

❖ Drastic changes in hormone levels

❖ Sore throat

If you are having problems with the throat chakra closing, try not to be so hard on yourself. You may have past experiences where it was painful to communicate such as a harsh argument that has stuck with you. You could also have difficulty with opening this chakra is you were told as a child to keep your feelings to yourself.

Ether is the element for the throat chakra. Sitting in a space where you can enjoy the clear sky will remove the blocked energy. Alternatively, eat blue foods such as dragon fruit, currants and blueberries.

Day 13 Throat Chakra Physical Meditation

1.　Sit in a comfortable position on a yoga mat, cushion or chair. Place your feet flat on the floor if you are sitting in a chair.

2.　Close your eyes and breathe in three smooth and deep breaths in through your nose and out through your mouth.

3.　Focus your concentration on your breathing and the flow throughout your body.

4.　As you exhale, pay special attention to the sound of the breath entering and exiting your body.

5.　Continue your focus on your breath between three to five minutes, noting the sensations of the air in the throat.

6.　When you have completed your allotted time, slowly open your eyes and get up slowly to your feet.

Day 14 Throat Chakra Mental Meditation

1.	Sit down in a comfortable chair with a straight back in a place you will not be disturbed.

2.	Inhale and exhale ten times smooth and deep. Breathe in through your nose and exhale through your mouth.

3.	Starting at the top of your head, mentally scan down the body and imagine your muscles relaxing as pass your body over.

4.	When your muscles are relaxed, envision a spinning, vibrant blue ball at your throat chakra.

5.	Imagine the sphere is growing larger and brighter.

6.	As it grows, imagine your throat chakra expanding and clearing at the same time.

7.	Allow the blue energy to take over the energy of all your body.

8.	Sit with this energy, continuing to focus on your breath between three and five minutes.

9.	When you are done, slowly open your eyes and take your time getting back to your feet.

Day 15 Throat Chakra Spiritual Meditation

1.   Sit comfortably in a meditation posture which is comfortable for you. This can be on a yoga mat, cushion or a chair.

2.   Close your eyes and take in three normal breaths, focusing on the flow of the air throughout your body.

3.   Concentrate upon the spine at your neck as you envision blue throughout your sight of vision.

4.   Take note how the color makes you feel.

5.   Focus the blue into a sphere at your throat chakra at the spine.

6.   As you breathe in, focus your concentration on the sphere as you say "hum" pronounced like humming.

7.   Release the breath as you envision the blue sphere vibrating as the air passes through your throat.

8.   With each breathe, see the sphere getting larger and more vibrant.

9.   Continue chanting between three and five minutes as you continue to concentrate on the throat chakra vibrations.

10.   As you breathe in, fill yourself with positive energies. Allow the breath as it exits your body to take away any of the

blockages and tension that you feel.

11.   When the exercise is complete, slowly open your eyes and take your time moving when you are comfortable to do so.

Chapter 19 The Third Eye Reiki Meditation Day Sixteen Through Eighteen

Overview of the Ajna Chakra - Third Eye or 6th Chakra

he 6th chakra is associated with the element of light and gives the person imagination, vision, wisdom, guidance and insight when it is clear and charged. The pineal gland, forehead and eyes are associated with the third eye chakra. It is where our sixth sense and

intuition reside and is associated with the color of indigo.

The ajna chakra is the seat of the hormones for wakefulness and sleep are released as the area between your eyebrows is sensitive to the light of day and the absence of light in the darkness. When you continue to work with the 6th chakra, you will become more empathic and sensitive towards the feelings of others and also the universe.

Continued work to clear and charge this chakra will also the Kundalini Shakti to open and close your third eye to give you insight into situations as needed. When it is balanced, you will know all the answers that you need to know when you need to know them. There is no need to search outwardly for answers. You will simply know intuitively as you will trust your higher consciousness fully. However, if this chakra is not balanced, you will have a difficult time of making decisions which are clear and to your highest benefit.

Ranging from the root chakra at the bottom of the spine to the crown chakra at the top of the head, all seven chakras are powerful energy centers.

The aim is to use chakra exercises to keep all these energy centers open and balanced. If you can achieve this, you'll be better able to fulfill your full potential and live a happy life. In contrast, the more chakras are blocked or misaligned, the more you'll sense something is wrong.

Responsibilities of the Third Eye Chakra

Your third eye chakra is situated between your eyebrows and is your direct connection to your spirituality. It has an affect on the following:

❖ Your feeling of being stuck, stagnant or moving forward

* Your balance between reason and emotion

* Your ability to see the bigger picture of life

* Your capability to form accurate gut feelings

Imbalance Symptoms

With your 6th chakra in balance, you will be able to make big decisions based on a balance of logic and emotions. You will have a solid trust in your intuition and know that you are living your purpose in life. Because you trust your intuition, you will naturally flow towards opportunities which are right for you and to your highest purpose. You will also be more mindful about yourself and the world around you. When the third eye is closed, you will doubt your intuition or the existence of it which will make you question everything. Other common symptoms include:

* Feel as if the weight of the world is on their shoulders alone and feel responsible

* Mood swings due to taking on other people's moods

* Paranoia

* Believing that your life or career is insignificant

* General indecisiveness

* Lack of faith within yourself or your purpose

- ❖ Sinus pain

- ❖ Leg and back pain

- ❖ Eye discomfort

- ❖ Migraines or headaches

- ❖ Trouble sleeping or insomnia

- ❖ Struggle to learn new concepts

- ❖ Clumsy

- ❖ Cynicism

- ❖ Overly logical or emotional

- ❖ Often lost in your thoughts

- ❖ Frequently escape into daydreaming to avoid reality

- ❖ Addicted to external things such as shopping, status, money, sex, food or relationships which you believe will bring you happiness

- ❖ Interactions with other people are very trivial or superficial

- ❖ Mistrust or dislike people easily

- ❖ Stubbornness

❖   Suffer from delusions or mental illness

You may find that your chakra becomes closed after someone belittles your passion or career. Also instances of transitions in life such as divorce, job loss, death or illness will cause a misalignment.

This chakra is coupled with light. To heal this chakra, sit in a sunny window or in the direct sunlight. Indigo foods such as blackberries, grapes and purple kale will help as well.

Day 16 Third Eye Chakra Physical Meditation

1.   Go outside in a place you will not be disturbed where you are able to see the moon clearly.

2.   Sit down in a comfortable position and take a few deep and long breaths. Breathe in through the nose and out through your mouth.

3.   Relax the muscles in your body and sink into the earth.

4.   Gaze upon the moon for as long as possible without blinking your eyes. As you gaze, envision the moon as an experience occurring within you.

5.   Become one with the energy of the moon as you feel it reverberating within you.

6.   Once this occurs, close your eyes slowly and focus your eyes upwards to the third eye. You should still see an image of the moon. If not, take in 5 long and deep breaths and focus on the movement of air in your body.

7.   When the image of the moon disappears from your mind's eye, open your eyes once again to gaze upon the moon.

8.   This is one round. Keep repeating as many times as necessary to practice this exercise for a minimum of 15 minutes until you are feeling too much strain in your eyes.

Day 17 Third Eye Chakra Mental Meditation

1.   Sit comfortably and close your eyes. Inhale and exhale ten times, slowly and deeply.

2.   Focus your attention on the location of the third eye chakra, imagine a violet sphere of energy in the middle of your forehead. Remember, purple is the third eye chakra's color.

3.   As you continue to breathe slowly and deeply, picture the purple ball of energy getting bigger and

warmer. As it does, imagine it purging negativity from your body.

4.   Think of yourself of absorbing the third eye chakra's energy—allow yourself to feel it all over.

5.   Open your eyes when you feel ready.

Day 18 Third Eye Chakra Spiritual Meditation

1.   Sit comfortably in a meditation posture which is comfortable for you. This can be on a yoga mat, cushion or a chair.

2.   Close your eyes and take in three normal breaths, focusing on the flow of the air throughout your body.

3.   Envision a white colored disk of energy rotating slowly at the top of your head.

4.   Imagine a violet ray of light reaching up to the sky.

5.   Then envision an additional violet beam coming from the sky to your white disk.

6.   Allow this violet beam to flow downwards through each chakra down to the muladhara and into the earth.

7.   Concentrate upon the light and let it envelop your entire body.

8.   Chant "Shaam" as you are exhaling.

9. Meditate on this energy for 20 minutes.

10. When you are done, slowly open your eyes and take your time getting back to your feet.

Chapter 20 Crown Chakra Reiki Meditation Day Nineteen Through Twenty-one

Overview of the Sahasrara Chakra - Crown or 7th Chakra

The crown chakra is located at the very top of the head and encompasses the elements of all of the chakras. It is associated with spirituality, communication with the Divine, union, ideas, awareness, thought, consciousness and nothingness which includes

everything. The part of the body which are affected by the 7th chakra are the nervous system, brain and head.

Since the sahasrara chakra is where Kundalini Shakti reunites with infinite wisdom, it is the last element in completing your Kundalini awakening. When the prana and Kundalini flow through to your 7th chakra, there is a blossoming of your consciousness. The color of this chakra is violet and leads to love-infused prana. As this energy is flowing, the pineal gland is further activated which leads to a vibrating feeling at the top of the head.

When this chakra is open, clear and balanced, Kundalini Shakti is able to freely flow and you will be connected to the divine source within you. It is the final step of the process. However, you will need to continue to work on keeping your chakras clear and charged to allow this prana to continuously flow. However, for this state of being, it is rather difficult to keep up with daily tasks in the West as we know it.

Responsibilities of the Crown Chakra

The 7th chakra is located at the top of your head, which is why it is known also as the crown chakra. It is your source of spiritual connectivity and has an influence on the following:

❖ Self-worth

❖ Capability of finding peace

❖ Restful sleep

❖ Motivation to reach goals

❖ Excitement levels

❖ The level of beauty you see in the world around you.

Imbalance Symptoms

When your crown chakra is in alignment, you will experience a high level of pleasure in life. You will experience joy and gratitude along with spiritual awareness. When your 7th chakra is out of balance, you will likely experience issues with restless, melancholy, boredom and disillusionment. Other symptoms of an overactive crown chakra are the following:

❖ Self-destructive habits

❖ Disconnect from your spirituality

❖ Apathy

❖ Cynicism

❖ Desire to oversleep

❖ Lack of inspiration

❖ Confusion on which direction you should take in life

❖ Exhaustion

❖ Chronic tension headaches

❖ Poor coordination

❖ Depression

There are several reasons why your crown chakra can become blocked. Some common ways are coined as mid-life crises when you are reevaluating components of your life such as your relationship or career.

Other ways are conflict in family relationships and negative feedback on projects that you are proud of.

Because this is the top chakra, it incorporates all of the aforementioned elements of earth, water, fire, air, ether and light. To balance out the energy of the crown chakra, spend quiet time in prayer, chanting mantras and meditation. There are no necessary changes needed for the diet.

Day 19 Crown Chakra Physical Meditation

1.   Sit in a comfortable position where you will not be disturbed. Keep your back straight and your legs uncrossed. Place your hands on your your upper legs with your palms facing upwards.

2.   Close your eyes and breath in through your nose and out through your mouth in three long and deep breaths.

3.   Ponder upon a problem or personal blockage that needs attention. Visualize this problem in your mind.

4. Start chanting "Om" as you exhale. Become one with the energy that you start to feel.

5. Envision a white ball of flame in the heart chakra. With each breath, see this light get brighter and larger to envelop your entire body.

6. Continue to focus on the breath as this white flame spreads at a minimum of three feet from your body on all sides.

7. Now visualize a small violet colored flame by starting in the same fashion as you created the white flame. You will cover this white flame with the violet flame when you are complete.

8. Repeat the intention "I AM the Violet Flame of presence, blazing and transforming whatever within me that needs to be healed." Repeat this intention as many times as you need.

9. Feel the sensation of the energy throughout your being and continue to focus on your breath.

10. When you have finished, slowly open your eyes and stand slowly back on your feet.

Day 20 Crown Chakra Mental Meditation

1.   Get comfortable while sitting in a chair with your back straight and your feet on the floor.

2.   Put your hands in your lap overlapping each other and turn your palms to the sky.

3.   Close your eyes and inhale through your nose and exhaling through your mouth.

4.   Envision a lotus flower at the top of your head.

5.   Continue to breathe slowly and evenly and see the lotus petals unfurling. There is a vibrant violet light in the middle of the lotus.

6.   Focus on your breathing as you see the light getting brighter and more vibrant.

7.   Feel the sensation of warmth at the crown of your head.

8.   Allow the warmth to flow downwards throughout your whole body.

9.   Sit with the sensations of warmth and continue to focus on your breath for ten minutes.

10.   open your eyes and sit quietly for a few minutes before you get back up on your feet.

Day 21 Crown Chakra Spiritual Meditation

1.   Sit comfortably in a meditation posture which is comfortable for you. This can be on a yoga mat, cushion or a chair.

2.   Close your eyes and take in three normal breaths, focusing on the flow of the air throughout your body.

3.   Bring your hands up to your face and cover your closed eyelids with the middle and ring fingers.

4.   Place your index finger on your eyebrows and your pinky fingers on your cheekbones.

5.   Breathe in deeply through the nose. As you exhale, chant "Om" with the "m" being drawn out, creating a buzzing sound.

6.   Continue meditating and chanting for five minutes.

7.   When the exercise is complete, slowly lower your hands and open your eyes. Take your time moving when you are comfortable to do so.

Chapter 21 Daily Practical Tips

It can seem like a daunting task at times when you get into a negative cycle of thinking to snap yourself out of it. Many times, empaths feel like they need to rant to express the pent up collection of emotions that

they are feeling. Sometimes there just does not seem like any other way to feel balanced and sane again. However, this is not always the best approach.

Ideally, you will try to keep negativity out of your life altogether as you realize that it does not serve you and only brings your mind and energy down to a low level. How are you able to be the best you can be when you are feeling miserable? Of course, you can use the self-care tools which are in chapter 4. However, there are further measures you can take to ensure that negativity does not cloud your energy and ultimately your day.

Center Yourself in Love and Truth

When you are not centered in your energy, this gives the person that you are interacting with the perfect opportunity to take advantage of syphoning your energy from you. The ego in the other person is driven to be fed and will drain you of your energy at any given moment as the ego is very selfish.

Signs that you are not centered are you will start to react to things that happen either in a conversation with another or a scenario that has happened in your environment. When you realize that you are reacting, especially out of emotion, you need to take a moment to recenter your energy.

Deep breathing exercises and meditations will help you to continue to stay in your calm, loving and true center. When you start to practice these daily, you will notice that you will not be as reactive with people or situations, and you will not become as drained and drawn to the negativity.

When you practice these centering activities, you are noticing your actions and thoughts from an impartial standpoint. It is as if you are seeing yourself from outside of your body. You are in a higher place and can see things for what they are. When you are in this state, you have achieved a balance based in love and truth. The longer you stay in this space, the deeper the connection will be with your inner voice and intuition.

Do Not See the World in Black and White

When you try to figure out what is "right" and "wrong" you are fighting a losing battle. The ego comes in to play and makes you think that everything that you are doing everything right, even if your gut tells you otherwise. When you just accept things as they are and not try to figure out what is right from an intellectual standpoint, you will be able to listen to what your intuition is trying to tell you to do.

This also means that you should not try to figure out the reasoning for negativity in another person's ego. When you start down this path, it will only start to feed your ego or their ego will start to drain your energy. Instead, continue to focus on your true purpose and determine if this person needs to be spending any more time with you.

If their ego is starting to go in a negative way by extending guilt, shame, blame or even start attacking you and your purpose, simply take note. Do not engage or react. This is exactly what the other person's ego wants as it will take the opportunity to take more energy from you.

Save Your Energy

When you are navigating through another person's emotions while you are not centered, you will certainly start to feel depleted of your energy. When you start to feel your energy start to dip, fill yourself up with light in every way possible. This should be done on an emotional, mental and physical way. Not only will it protect your energy from continuing to be drained, it will lift your spirits higher. Soon, your energy will be one that does not resonate with the energy vampire, and they will likely leave.

When you are able to save your energy from people who are trying to take advantage of you, this leaves you available for the people who need your help and will appreciate it. They will not willingly take your light and energy away; they will welcome it. You will also see the benefit in helping and talking with people who are only wanting to lift each other up higher.

You Come First

Allowing yourself to come first is quite effective when utilized on a regular basis. When you make sure that you practice your self-care each day and you ensure that your needs are met each day, this will prioritize your energy to where it needs to flow.

Remember, you are only able to be an effective psychic when your energy is centered and balanced. When you do not put your needs first, your time and energy will likely be spent on other people's needs. You will not be able to find the balance that you need while experiencing the world as a psychic or sensitive person in this way.

Effective Practices to Protect Yourself from Negativity

When you have negative energy attached to your body, there are several signs to warn you which are:

Negative thinking
Mood swings and emotions being uncontrollable uncharacteristic impulsiveness

Headaches and stomachaches that will not go away Inability to sleep

Feeling of restlessness

Feeling of depression, anxiousness or simply down

Suddenly feeling drained or tired

Not feeling like doing your regular routine

No matter where we go, there is negative energy which can infiltrate our energy levels and bodies. They can come from people or environments and it makes you feel more negative even when there is no immediate cause. When the dense energy affects your energy levels, you may feel a dip in your alertness and productivity. When it is found in your body, you will start to have physical symptoms such as headaches or pains throughout the body which cannot be readily explained.

Luckily, there are many different methods that can be used singularly or in combination to help you to rid yourself of the negative energies and get you back into a good place.

Herbal Smudging Stick - You can utilize an herbal smudging stick which can be used on yourself and your immediate environment. They usually come small hand tied bundles of Sweetgrass, Cedar, Mugwart, Rosemary or the most popular White Sage. They can also be in the form of incense sticks as they are a more concentrated form of the herbal bundles.

Light the top of the herbal bundle or incense stick and move it in a circular motion so that the fire is put out and it is just smoking. Continue to circle around the body by motioning around each of your seven main chakras and then around your whole body. The power of intention is necessary to clear out any negative thoughts or energies. Just thinking about the dense energy leaving your body will free its grasp on you.

If you want to smudge your house, simply walk around each room and permeate the rooms with the smoke. Pay special attention to where stagnant energy will rest underneath furniture and in corners. It is helpful to open the windows so that it invites the negative energies to vacate the house. Again, visualize these energies dissipating from your space while you are performing the smudging.

Saying a Mantra or Protection Prayer - As there are many choices as to what prayers or mantras to say, choose one that resonates with you and stick with it during the times you are clearing your energy. When you switch back and forth between different mantras during a clearing session, it confuses the energy.

Recite this mantra with emphasis and belief. When you think that it might work, it will not gain the power that it requires to work. You must absolutely believe these prayers are going to work with no doubt in your mind. This is when they are able to do their most powerful work.

Before you start to say the mantra, ask for your higher power to protect and aid you in ridding your body and environment from this negative energy. Ask for the energy to leave your body and remind that it does not have any power over you. Then start to take deep and deliberate cleansing breaths while visualizing a bright white light in a bubble around your body.

Start to say the prayer or mantra while visualizing the negative energy leaving your body and space. Say this prayer until you feel a general peace about you. Continue to keep the white light around you during and after the session to continue to strengthen your energy field to protect against the negative energies coming back into your body.

Dissipate the Energy with Noise - Everything in the Universe is comprised of vibrations. Some are denser than others, but this also means that it can be affected by other vibrations. When the energy in the environment seems too dense, make noise with your hands or start drumming if able to dissipate this energy. It will introduce a new vibration and will force the denser energy to break apart. You can simply clap your hands three times or you can incorporate this clapping exercise into a dance if you choose to continue to raise your spirits.

Physically Remove the Negative Energy - Use your hands to physically take the energy out and off of your body. This is something that can easily be done anywhere and will work quickly to help rid yourself of the negativity. Simply place your hands with your fingers together and move your hand across your body in a diagonal fashion. While you are doing this, visualize dusting this energy off of your body.

Use Protective Visualization - In the middle of your chest, picture a ball of golden light while you are taking deep breaths in and out. While you are breathing, imagine this ball of light growing larger with each breath you take in.

Expand this golden light until it covers your entire body and then approximately three feet away from the body on all sides to protect your aura.

Take a Bath or Shower - You can soak in a bath to release these dense energies from your body. Use a combination of 1 cup of baking soda with 1 cup of sea salt. You can mix this combination into a full bath or utilize this remedy while performing a foot bath by cutting the recipe into a quarter. Both will be effective in making your feel calmer, grounded and cleansed. If you are taking a shower, you can bundle some lavender or rose at the shower head to create a sweet and calming effect.

The Power of Thought - What you think becomes your life. When you focus and stress about all the things that are not making you happy in life, then you will only bring more stressful events into your life. Instead, shift your thinking to be more grateful for the things that you do have which make your life that much easier. Even look at the simple things as they will compound much easier. When you shift your thinking, you will automatically clear the negative energy in your body and around you as these two types of energy cannot coexist.

Remove the Negative People - When you find that you are constantly feeling drained about a certain person or group, you need to think about the positive benefits these people are bringing to your life compared to the negative effects. Usually, the good will not outweigh the bad in these instances when the negative effect is very great. Instead, find more positive and happy people to spend your time with as you become like the four people you are closest to your life.

Take A Walk - Dense energies literally drain away your energy and make you want to stay stagnant. When you become active, the negative energy will have less of a hold on you. It can be as simple as going for a short walk to help clear your head or going on a day trip to your favorite place to spend some me time.

Mindful Meditation - When you are feeling stressed out or pulled in too many directions, find a quiet place to sit and start breathing in several deep and intentional breaths. With each inhalation, imagine you are taking in the power of your higher source and then breathing out the negativity you want to rid yourself of. When you are feeling more grounded, start to clear your mind of all random thoughts until you find peace. This may take a few minutes or an hour, but it will calm your energy as well as clear the negativity away.

Just Let it Go - When you hold grudges or negative ideas about places and people, it takes a toll on your body. These emotions will attach onto you if you allow them to. However, if you simply let these emotions go when they appear, they will not have this hold on your and not infiltrate your energy field. Acknowledge how you are feeling but do not internalize the emotions. Simply breath and visualize these emotions floating away if they do get attached.

Get Moving - This can include any type of exercise to include running or even dancing. Moving your body helps to invigorate the organs in the body as the blood starts to flow. Stagnant energy cannot be present when you are on the move which will keep negative energy from clutching onto you. Also, you are getting a little healthier each time you get out while doing something that you enjoy.

Music Cures Everything - Put on your favorite tunes which help to lift your spirit. Try to refrain from any depressing music. Feel the pulsing go through your body as it energizes your system and start to feel more upbeat. Find some new music who are similar to other artists that you enjoy to broaden your music collection and find songs that have positive lyrics and messages.

Sincere Gratitude - Just as positivity and negativity cannot exist in the same space, if you practice gratitude for what you have in your life, this

will dissipate negative thoughts and energy. Consider writing down the people and events that you are thankful for. If you are having difficulty coming up with things to write, ponder about how there are many people in the world who are much worse off than you. When you understand that everyone in life goes through ups and downs, it helps you realize the bigger picture.

Inner Child Nurturing - Act and play with your inner child by putting your favorite happy song on the stereo system and sing at the top of your lungs. Even better if you dance along as if no one is watching. When you let yourself go in this positive way, the negative energy will lift very quickly. If singing is not your thing, find some silly jokes online or a favorite funny video.

Let Nature Shine - If your house or office is feeling negative and stagnant, open the windows or doors and let the breeze bring some new air and energy into the space. The sunshine will also couple well with the new air and you will feel revitalized, keeping negativity at bay.

Conclusion

I hope you enjoyed your copy of Chakra Meditation: 21 Days Guided Meditation to Awaken your Spiritual Power, Reduce Stress & Anxiety and Improve Awareness of Psychic Abilities with Reiki Healing

Exercises. Let us hope it gave you all of the information that you were searching for about how to use Reiki and meditation techniques to heal yourself as well what you needed to get started in delving into the psychic abilities that we all possess.

The next step is to start working on the exercises which are going to strengthen your intuitive and psychic skills which will continue to compound into enjoyed benefits. There is no reason to be discouraged about your particular talents. When you continue to work with embracing and appreciating yourself for being a unique human being, the more confident and comfortable in your skin you will become.

When you are starting to apply the knowledge in this book, it is best to write down what your particular goals are so that you will have direction and not be side tracked. When you start to work with each goal individually, you will come to master your skills and goals at a higher rate. It will also help to keep you motivated towards the reasons you started in the first place.

Remember to keep your energies and thoughts balanced so that you do not feel overwhelmed. Utilize the methods in having more control over what emotions and sensations that you experience so that you are able to continue to fortify your skills. When you use this book to have more understanding about yourself, you will become your greatest self which will be able to help others much deeper than what you are capable of now.

Once you make it through the initial 21 days of the reiki meditation, be sure to keep it going. Take note where you body is still having issues, and work with the corresponding chakra. Keeping your energy clear and clean is an ongoing process, but you will know where and what to do now when a problem arrises.

When you finally start to embrace yourself for the beautiful soul that you are, you will start to realize all the benefits and gifts that come with living your life truly connected. Other than growing into a strong, deeper and connected individual, you will make a large impact in your family, community and even the world with your talents. The sky is the limit, and only you are limiting yourself in this matter.

I wish you luck while you continue down your paths in your journey. Remember to always trust your intuition as it will never steer you wrong, and have faith that you will be able to master all aspects of your psychic abilities so that you will shine at your brightest at all times. Also keep up with the meditation practices as they will continue to benefit you for some time to come.

Finally, if you found this book useful in any way, a review on Amazon is always appreciated! Thank you!

Reiki Healing

An Essential Guide For Beginners To Learn To Self-Healing With Positive Spiritual Energy By Using Traditional Techniques Of Yoga Therapy And Chakras Meditation.

by

New Mindfulness Lab